THE
Power
OF
Archetypes

THE
Power
OF
Archetypes

How to Use Universal Symbols to
Understand Your Behavior
and Reprogram Your
Subconscious

MARIE D. JONES

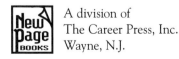
A division of
The Career Press, Inc.
Wayne, N.J.

THE POWER OF ARCHETYPES
Edited by Roger Sheety
Typeset by Kara Kumpel
Cover design by Howard Grossman/12E Design
Cover image by agsandrew/depositphotos
Printed in the U.S.A.

To order this title, please call toll-free 1-800-CAREER-1 (NJ and Canada: 201-848-0310) to order using VISA or MasterCard, or for further information on books from Career Press.

The Career Press, Inc.
12 Parish Drive
Wayne, NJ 07470
www.careerpress.com

Library of Congress Cataloging-in-Publication Data

Dedicated to Max:
Hero, Warrior, Sage.

"Until you make the unconscious conscious,
it will direct your life and you will call it fate."
—Carl Jung

[acknowledgments]

I would like to thank my wonderful agent, Lisa Hagan of Lisa Hagan Literary Agency, for being my longtime champion, fearless word warrior, and amazing friend. I would also like to thank the entire staff at New Page Books, most notably Michael Pye and Laurie Pye, for allowing me to express my ideas on paper year after year. You guys are the best, every single one of you! Lauren, Gina, Jeff, Adam, Allison, Roger, Diana, and the entire crew—you make the coolest books a reality! I hope I didn't leave anyone out!

I must thank my friends and family for being so supportive and forgiving of how much time I spend writing, or thinking about writing, from my mom, Milly; sister, Angella; brother, John; and extended family (Dad in heaven!), and my good pals Wendy, Therese, Jan, and Stephanie for the great times and laughter that keep me sane! I also cherish the many readers and fans I have made through the years with my books, radio shows, television shows, and online via social networking. To the great friends I have met online, and to my colleagues and fellow writers everywhere, thanks for the constant inspiration! Without you guys, who would listen to me? Well...

The one person I wish to thank the most is my son, Max. He is the moon, stars, and sun all rolled together, and the perfect example of the archetypes of warrior, hero, and sage, with the occasional trickster sneaking in for good measure. Without Max, my own hero's journey would be so much less meaningful.

[contents]

[introduction]

All over the world, there are universal symbols understood by every culture, religion, class system, race, and creed. These symbols are powerful subconscious drivers of our understanding and perception of the world we live in and the forces we interact with, as well as who we are as individuals. The actual definition of the word "archetype" is an idea or original pattern/model from which all things of the same type are representations or copies. The ancient Greek root of the word is *archein*, meaning "original, old," and *typos* meaning "pattern, type, model."[1] Thus, an archetype is an original pattern from which all other similar persons, objects, ideas, concepts, and themes are derived, copied, modeled, and emulated.

In Jungian psychology, an archetype is an inherent idea or mode of thought derived from the experience of the species/race and present in the individual and collective unconscious. Carl Gustav Jung, the famed psychologist, utilized these symbols as a means for understanding the path to personal enlightenment, the way the world works, the way the human psyche works, and how to empower, heal, or achieve goals and desires. There are human and animal archetypes; in fact, Jung once said there were as many archetypes as there are typical situations in life, that they constructed a type of formula for the functioning of the subconscious, and they have the distinct characteristic of showing up throughout human history in the same form, with the same meaning. He defined 12 in particular that played a large role in the development of our psyches and personalities.

An archetype is the same anywhere around the globe, no matter what culture, religion, geographical boundary, or language spoken, for it represents the language of the collective detached from the intellect and judgment of the conscious mind. Often, we don't even think about how we got to behave, act, and think the way we do or what molded our personalities until something happens, usually tragic, that makes us realize we are not happy, fulfilled expressions of our deepest selves. This is where archetypes can be an incredible learning tool.

Common archetypes include:

The Hero: sent on a quest to pursue his/her destiny. Comparative mythologist Joseph Campbell spoke and wrote extensively of the "hero's journey" found in many great novels and movies, including *Star Wars*.

The Self: our individual persona seeking to become completely realized, usually via the hero's journey.

The Shadow Self: our opposing, amoral, instinctual, and primitive side associated with the past.

Mentor: the main guide of the self on its journey.

The Persona: the masks we wear to show others and hide who we truly are.

Anima/Animus: our female and male psyches, roles, and desires.

God: the perfected self.

Goddess: Mother Earth.

Trickster: the change agent.

Beast: the primitive past of humanity.

Sage: the wise ones among us.

Mother: the nurturer.

Father: the protector.

Wizard: the one who knows how to transform and who has hidden knowledge we seek.

The Fool: our confused, faulty self.

Scapegoat: the one we assign blame to.

These are just a sampling of the many archetypes we may already be familiar with, including the enemy/adversary/Devil, who often stands in the way of the hero achieving his/her mission and, thus, destiny. Because Jungian archetypes are often used to help understand a spiritual and hidden dimension to our existence, they can also help to explain a layout of that dimension, and give us insight and guidance as to how to overcome any obstacles or blocks we face on our journey. But Jung was not the only person to develop a list of archetypes. We now have so many others to work with who can help empower us in ways even Jung may not have imagined, all existing in the deepest parts of who we are as human beings.

Jung posited that the collective unconscious was akin to a storehouse of information, myths, stories, and symbols that all humans have access to, and is a necessary part of the human psyche. Especially during times of conflict, the collective unconscious can be tapped into for wisdom, guidance, and understanding, and also may be the realm of angels, spirits, demons, and other guardians and helpers that exist apart from our manifest reality, such as the spirit guides visited by shamans during their drumming journeys.

Think of the collective unconscious as a universal reservoir that allows all humans to quench their subjective, symbolic thirst for meaning, especially when it comes to those things that are not objective, empirical, or direct experiences. Thus, any symbolic theme in that reservoir can ease the thirst of any culture, albeit in different modes of expression on the surface (think of using a blue cup dipped in a sink as opposed to a green cup—you get the same water, but via a different colored cup).

This book looks at the history and meaning of archetypes, and their use in literature, philosophy, and psychology. But it also takes a deeper look at how these shared symbols of the subconscious can play out in our daily lives, for better or worse, and how we have the power to use them to both our detriment and advantage. As millions of people flock to television shows like *The Walking Dead* and *Game of Thrones*, or movies like the *Star Wars* franchise, they may be totally unaware of the powerful attraction these characters have over them. The book will take several examples of our popular culture to dissect the archetypes present in each character, and why we become such rabid fans. It's all about what is happening in our subconscious mind as we view these shows and fall in love, or hate, with these characters!

Understanding the different aspects of our psyche, our persona, is what archetypes allow us to do, empowering us to take control of how we let them manifest in our love relationships, finances, career goals, health, and happiness. Just as Joseph Campbell wrote in *The Hero's Journey* of the archetypes we encounter as we journey through life, this book will look at the many possible functions these symbols serve, both individually and collectively, as a society and a species.

Archetypes are indicators of the stories of our lives and the good news is that once we become aware of them, we can work with and even change them to tell a different, more empowering story. The book will offer tips, tools, and exercises specifically designed to help the reader create that new story, as well as insights from people in the fields of psychology, recovery, and spiritual growth who use archetypes in their own work to help others heal, grow, and succeed in life. It also features intriguing glimpses into the minds of writers who create characters often based upon archetypes that resonate with readers. We will see how we are all influenced by these symbols in our popular culture, our politics, our religious traditions, and our relationships with others.

Each of us, by changing and working with our own individual archetypes, can change our own lives. By doing that, we begin to add to the collective to create a more loving, empowering, and compassionate world to counteract the symbols of evil and greed, power and corruption. It's all about putting archetypes to use at home and in the world to shift the paradigm.

And it all begins…within.

[chapter 1]

The Multilayered Mind

Before we can learn to change our minds and, therefore, our lives, we must understand how our minds work. Not knowing this keeps us trapped in old default patterns, programs, and plotlines we didn't mean to write, but were written for us. The problem is we focus too much on the conscious mind and what it reveals to us, and not enough on the deeper levels, where the real work is being done behind the scenes, shaping who we are, what we think we want and need, and how we view ourselves out there in the bigger world. We believe we are single-minded when the truth is we have many aspects to our mind.

We live life consciously aware of everything around us, certain that our perceptions of reality are complete based upon this awareness. The mind sees, hears, feels, smells, and tastes; it makes choices, decisions, and assumptions based on the collected data that is processed in the brain. To be consciously aware is to be alive and functioning. This is our waking state, where we take things at face value by the sheer fact that we can experience them with one or more of our five senses.

Unbeknownst to most of us is the fact that a very large part of our reality comes from a deeper level of consciousness where symbols are the chosen language and information is shrouded and veiled in subtleties and vagaries, left for the conscious mind to interpret—if it is even aware enough to know how to interpret them correctly. The idea that what drives our actions, behaviors, personalities, desires, and psyches comes from the conscious mind is somewhat false. In fact, there is ongoing debate as to exactly how many levels of the mind we use to create, perceive, and even manifest the "real world."

Some scholars and scientists say we have three minds: conscious, subconscious, and unconscious. Others group the subconscious and unconscious into one for the sake of simplicity. Others still add on two other critical levels, as we shall see. All of these work together to create the personalities and identities we call our own.

Conscious Mind

Our waking state is the world of the conscious mind. This is the state of awareness of our environment and how we interact with it. One might say being conscious means being able to function, using our minds to think, process information, retain and recall memories, and formulate perceptions based upon our surroundings. To be conscious is to be engaged in life with some or all of our five senses, and to interact with others, too.

Imagine an iceberg. The tip of that iceberg is the part visible above the surface of the ocean. Though it may be 100 feet high, the part of the iceberg below the surface is massive in comparison. The conscious mind is the tip of the iceberg of the totality of who we are. It's just the tip and yet we tend to focus on the conscious mind as being primary to the forces and influences that make up our personalities and drive our choices and decisions.

Because we exist in a visual culture, what we "see" on the surface is what we think is most important. Because we cannot see below the surface of the water, we tend to give less importance to the functioning of the remaining parts of the mind. This is a huge mistake when it comes to understanding how we, as human beings, perceive ourselves, others, and everything around us. But we are programmed to do so.

The conscious mind exists in the present moment, although we do spend quite a bit of its time dwelling on the past and the future. The conscious mind likes to think it's in charge, and that it is very linear, objective, and empirical. It demands proof. It has to see it to believe it. It's like a bully when it comes to understanding the truth about things, because it insists on going with what it sees on a surface level only, often ignoring messages and intuitions that come from deeper levels of the mind.

When we think of our lives and ourselves, we do so from the conscious mind. We plan and move toward goals. We see ourselves in a certain way and take actions based on that vision. We behave in accordance with external influences, assumptions, and expectations so that we can put forth the best face possible. We create the story of our life with tangibles, the stuff we can grasp onto that appears to be real. The conscious mind drives our lives and determines our destinies. It is the "what you see is what you get" mind.

Those who have told us that we are what we think about all day long are only partially correct. We are probably more what we don't think about—at least not consciously. Beneath the tip lies the massive body of the iceberg, where powerful forces are at work shaping our personalities and personal storylines.

That our thoughts, conscious behaviors, and actions are responsible for the life we are now living, the good, bad, and ugly, is the biggest lie we can ever tell ourselves, because the truth is that the conscious mind is more of a reactor than a creator, more responder than activator. It is more imposed upon than it imposes upon. This is why so many people live lives that are unsatisfying, unfulfilling, dull, inauthentic, and well, "lifeless." It's because they are operating from the conscious mind, and that is not the realm of dreams, inspiration, or the desire to express authenticity and truth. The conscious mind is the realm of will power, intellect, thought, surface self-knowledge, factual understanding, deliberation, alertness to environment, processing of information and data, objectivity, ego identity, and present moment awareness. It takes perceptions and gives them interpretations, meaning, and a place within our accepted world view. Usually those interpretations are limited and based on our sensory input or thoughts, which we then accept as the truth of our reality.

This truth couldn't be further from the truth. We are told to "know thyself," but too often we stop seeking self-knowledge beyond what our conscious mind tells us, thinking we now understand why we are who we are!

So, what then is the level of the mind that lies beneath the surface of the ocean, dwarfing the conscious mind in size, power, and influence?

Subconscious Mind

Here is the base of that massive iceberg, the place where the actual activity occurs that helps us to process and perceive our personal and collective realities. We each have an iceberg, above and below the waterline. The subconscious mind is the powerhouse that is most responsible for things such as our emotions and emotional responses, intuition and gut feelings, habits and programming, memories and projections, subjective beliefs, and the imagination. Although we may have a conscious idea of who we think we are, the realm of the subconscious tells us who we really are through repeated behaviors and thoughts that often occur under the radar and make it very difficult to overcome or change them.

The subconscious might be described as the dumping ground for every perception, belief, idea, bit of information, and experience we've had since birth (maybe even before!) all churning below the surface, continuing to drive the trajectory of our lives long after the dumping occurred. It lies beyond our focal awareness and includes automatic processing responses to data and information that are not readily available to us in an immediate sense.

In the subconscious, all of our past programming, ideas, beliefs, thoughts, impressions, and assumptions exist in a kind of primordial soup from which the vast majority of our actions and behaviors are created. This soup is outside of our waking state, but we can indeed access it via things like deep meditation, hypnosis, and other methods of quieting the intellect and monkey mind to allow the deeper mind to speak its language.

The subconscious is rife with activity, constantly applying symbolic meaning to what we are experiencing on the surface, what our five senses are absorbing. Memories of the past live here, including those of the deep past, our childhoods, long ago, which may not be retrievable by the conscious mind unless a lot of hard work is applied, often with the use of trigger images, sounds, and smells to help activate them.

The subconscious sees and notices everything, even if the conscious mind doesn't register it. Imagine sitting with a friend having lunch and a pink, polka-dotted Volkswagen Bug drives by. Because you are so immersed in what your friend is telling you, your conscious mind doesn't even notice the goofy car, but if someone later asked if you saw the crazy VW Bug driving around town, you would remember it and possibly in great detail. You didn't even notice it, but your subconscious took a very detailed "picture" of it that is now imprinted upon your memory and stored in the warehouse forever.

Many psychologists and scientists state that up to 90 percent of our personality, beliefs, and behaviors originate from subconscious programming that we are usually not even aware is running. It's like having a computer on all the time, running programs in the background, while we are busy focused on other things, and we don't realize those background programs are literally driving all of our thoughts, emotions, actions, and moods. Without knowing this, we look for conscious or external things to try to fix what isn't working in our lives. If we are unhappy, we try to "figure it out" using the intellect and rationalization, and then we wonder why we still can't change or make our situations better.

It's because the subconscious is running the show, leaving little wiggle room for the conscious mind to redirect our habits and behaviors toward those that will better serve us. How could it, when it has no idea why we are the way we are, or why we do the things we do? Have you ever tried to quit being a codependent or lose weight and exercise more on sheer, conscious willpower alone? Some may succeed at going it cold turkey, but for most people, even though they want to quit and know mentally and intellectually why they should, *they can't!* It's due to the subconscious "tapes" running continuously, influencing everything they feel, think, and do, and doing it "out of sight" so that they are not immediately identified as the reasons for failure and struggle.

Brian Tracy, author and motivational speaker, states on his website that the subconscious is like a huge memory bank, and that everything that happens to you is stored for all eternity in this massive and unlimited storehouse. By the time you reach the age of 21, he claims you've already stored more information than that found in the *Encyclopedia Britannica* one hundred times over! He says: "The function of your subconscious mind is to store and retrieve data. Its job is to ensure that you respond exactly the way you are programmed. Your subconscious mind makes everything you say or do fit a pattern consistent with your self-concept, your 'master program.'"[1]

Because this is a subjective part of the overall mind, the subconscious cannot think or perceive independently, and instead obeys any commands given by your conscious mind. You say you are feeling fat and ugly, and your subconscious accepts that as true, allowing that thought, however negative and untrue, to grow like a plant. "Your conscious mind commands, your subconscious mind obeys," Tracy says.[2]

If you attempt to do anything outside of the programming of the subconscious, or outside of your comfort zone, you will feel anxious and awful. But until the subconscious is examined, and reprogrammed if needed, you will continue to repeat the same patterns of action and activity again and again, for better and for worse.

The subconscious is also responsible, though, for keeping our bodies running via the homeostatic impulse, which keeps body temperature and pulse regulated and allows us to breathe and have a heartbeat without having to think about it or make it happen. It works with the automatic nervous system to make sure all our organs and parts are properly functioning—and we don't even have to consciously be aware of it or direct it.

So when we do recognize things we wish to change, we must first clear out the negative programming within this powerful and influential realm. Otherwise, our attempts at change won't stick, even if they are positive and would make us happy. We are, in some ways, like preprogrammed robots that repeat the same movements, patterns, and thought processes continuously until we go a bit deeper to see why.

Unconscious Mind (Personal)

Famed psychoanalyst Sigmund Freud, the founder of psychoanalytic theory, posited that the subconscious and the unconscious mind were one and the same. Although we may look at unconsciousness as being in a dangerous state of health, such as in a coma, he saw it as akin to the subconscious, in a realm below the surface mind where symbol, theme, and imagery prevailed. Freud's psychoanalytic view perceived the subconscious as responsible for the inner forces that direct our behavior and often result in slips of the tongue and verbal mistakes that are known as "Freudian slips" for their representation of the inner influencing the outer at the least likely of times.[3]

In the unconscious realm are thoughts, emotions, memories, desires, motivations, and all that does not exist in surface mind. But, like the subconscious, it is the main originator of our personalities and identities, or those we show to the external world. To Freud, this is a reservoir of often unacceptable and uncomfortable information we choose to suppress and deny, yet which continues to shape and mold us nonetheless.

Sigmund Freud

Known as the father of psychoanalysis, Sigmund Freud (1856–1939) was an accomplished man. In addition to being a psychologist, he was also a physiologist, a medical doctor, and a 20th century philosopher who posited and refined concepts of the human mind as a complex and layered system, as well as the concepts of infantile sexuality, sexual repression, the unconscious influence, and the use of understanding the levels of the mind in therapy. He was also the father of six children including his daughter Anna, who also became a psychoanalyst.

To Freud, the mind was broken down into the preconscious, conscious, and unconscious, and also, for psychoanalytic purposes, the id, ego, and superego. The id is the part of the mind that controls instinctual sexual drives and the desire for satisfaction. The superego is the conscience, which gives us socially acquired control mechanisms often first taught to us by our parents and later by our peers. The ego is the conscious self, created from the interactions of the id and superego, and tasked with reconciling conflicts between the two. The ego is the conscious mind, the id the unconscious, with the superego acting as a gatekeeper or screener to the unconscious.

This model of the mind was critical to much of his writings and research, as were his ideas of repressed sexuality as a driver of complex human behaviors and actions.

In the early 1900s, he published several books, including *The Interpretation of Dreams*, *The Psychopathology of Everyday Life*, and *Three Essays on the Theory of Sexuality*. His 1923 work, *The Ego and the Id*, explained his tripartite model of the mind that was to become a mainstay for his theories until his death in 1939.

Freud's theory of the unconscious is perhaps most important, as he helped lay the groundwork to our understanding of this hidden realm of power over our awakened mind. He believed the unconscious was deterministic and that mental and thought processes and states in the unconscious directly influenced the conscious level of behavior. What was repressed, including sexuality going back to infancy, in the unconscious could continue to manifest in behaviors and issues such as neuroses, obsessive behaviors, and even in dreams. Though Freud by many critical standards appeared focused on sexuality and sexual pleasure seeking as a driver of behavior, which served to separate one of his followers, Carl Gustav Jung, away and into his own field of psychoanalytic study, his understanding of the power of the unconscious mind and the role of the id, ego, and superego was foundational to our modern understanding of how therapeutic modalities work to help affect change by utilizing all levels of the mind, especially instinct, repressed memory, and emotion. Though many will remember him as obsessed with sexual drive as the most important force behind human behavior, the truth is, to Freud, sexual energy, or libido, was more about the life force and the pursuit of any pleasure, not just sexual. To him, human instinct and drive, both originating in the unconscious, were something we experienced from birth pushing us to achieve bodily pleasure, whether via sex, food, or even dancing!

The next time you experience a "Freudian slip" of the tongue, remember that it's not an accident. It's your unconscious speaking. Freud also believed that psychic events took place in the realm of the unconscious, such as symbolic dreams, intuitions, and urgings, which he suggested were akin to hidden messages from our unconscious mind to our conscious mind. Whether or not our conscious mind correctly interpreted those hidden messages, or followed through on them, was then in the hands of our intellect and will.

Importantly, the unconscious mind is not the same as being in a state of unconsciousness, such as when in a coma. This mistaken association may be why many modern therapists and psychoanalysts will refer to it as the subconscious, in order to emphasize the difference. Yet modern research is beginning to point to the possibility that people in comas are actually experiencing a state of consciousness different from the waking, functioning state. Though they may not have brain activity, they are aware and alive.[4,5,6]

For the sake of this book, we will use the term "subconscious" to represent this part of the mind because there is another, even deeper part that is referred to as the collective unconscious. To keep it less confusing, the subconscious will encompass the unconscious personal mind, the realm of stored information from the present, past, and distant past.

Although the subconscious/unconscious is most responsible for much of what exists in our minds, there is an even deeper level, far more vast and expansive, that is more likely the true origin point of our personalities and psyches. This realm, or level, influences the subconscious and conscious realms in mysterious but significant ways.

The Collective Unconscious

Going back to the iceberg analogy, the collective unconscious is *the water itself*, larger in size and more powerful and potent in its functions and implications. The water is all around the iceberg, keeping it afloat, affecting its size, shape, and melting and freezing rates during different kinds of weather.

The collective unconscious is the work of Carl Jung, who was a student and colleague of Freud's before breaking off to develop his own theories and directions in psychoanalysis.

Carl Gustav Jung

Born in 1875, of Swiss German descent, Carl Gustav Jung started in the fields of psychiatry and psychotherapy, and eventually founded the field of analytical psychology. He also was influential in the fields of archeology, anthropology, and even philosophy. His incredible body of work includes seminal books about consciousness, symbology, the collective unconscious, and archetypes, as well as dream interpretation and individuation—the process of integrating the conscious with the unconscious as a part of human development.

Early in his career, Jung was a solid supporter of Freud's theories and research, especially in their shared interest with the unconscious, but in 1912 he broke away from Freud's theories of infantile sexuality and the Oedipus complex. One of his main beefs was Freud's insistence that a person's past and especially their childhood experiences determined their future behavior. Jung agreed with this and added that humans are shaped by the future as well, namely by aspirations and desires. Jung also differed with Freud about the definition of libido. Freud focused on sexual energy, whereas Jung looked at libido as more generalized psychic energy.

Their differences prompted Jung to create his own theories, including that of the collective unconscious shared with all members of the human species.

Jung was an army doctor during World War I, married, and had five children. His wife, Emma, died in 1955, six years before Jung himself passed on. During his lifetime, he wrote such books as *Psychology of the Unconscious*; an autobiography, *Memories, Dreams, Reflections*; *The Archetypes and the Collective Unconscious*; *Flying Saucers: A Modern Myth of Things Seen In the Skies*; and *Psychology and Alchemy*, among others.

A huge proponent of art therapy and alchemy, especially in terms of symbolism, Jung's theory of psychological types was the foundation of the Myers-Briggs Type Indicator test. His influence is widespread even today in psychology, anthropology, religious studies, philosophy, metaphysics, New Age studies, consciousness studies and noetics, and even quantum physics![7,8]

Jung realized that behind the world's myths and origin stories were symbols that appeared universal to every region, creed, race, culture, and even between cultures that have never interacted with each other. These symbols were, in Jung's mind, thought to be the result of patterns in the unconscious that were of both genetic and non-genetic origin. These patterns are inherited by each generation, and exist in this reservoir of symbols and patterns called the collective unconscious.

As the storehouse of symbols and patterns, the collective unconscious can be accessed by anyone, with certain symbols or archetypes emerging into our conscious experience, depending on what is happening in our conscious world. This is also the realm of latent memories from our distant ancestors and distant past that are passed down through generations via genetic memory.

Jung believed there were actually two levels to the collective unconscious, but that the top, more surface level was actually the "personal unconscious," filled with elements based on our own personal, individual experiences. The collective level was underneath this. In *The Archetypes and the Collective Unconscious*, Jung writes, "this personal unconscious rests upon a deeper layer, which does not derive from personal experience and is not a personal acquisition, but is inborn."[9] This deeper layer is called the collective unconscious because "this part of the unconscious is not individual, but universal; in contrast to the personal psyche, it has contents and modes of behavior that are more or less the same everywhere and in all individuals." He goes on to liken it to a "common psychic substrate" that is more of a suprapersonal nature. It is present in every single one of us.[10]

Jung likened it to the "spiritual heritage of humanity as a whole," and that it was born in the brain structure of every new individual as a depository of ancient wisdom and knowledge, like a giant library of the experiences, ideas, and beliefs of our ancestors all the way back to the beginning of human existence on Earth. He also believed that mental illnesses could be linked to experiences embedded in the collective unconscious, as influences from other people in another time, and that to be healed it was a matter of reharmonizing the personality with the greater collective.[11]

The contents of this substrate are archetypes, which we will delve into in the next chapter. This layer of mind is the most important in determining past programming that even in our more aware and awake adult years can't seem to be overcome, even after we've done our lot of work on the conscious and subconscious. It is so deep that we may not be aware it's there or how it works to keep us within a confined box of ideals, beliefs, behavioral patterns and processes of thought, and reaction and response.

Superconscious

Finally, if the collective unconscious is the water, the superconscious is the air above the iceberg. This is the "God mind" or the higher mind in nonreligious terms. This is the part of the human mind posited to be directly linked to a higher intelligence that, depending on one's beliefs, exists within us, is external to us, or both. The superconscious transcends human consciousness and is our field of all possibility and potentiality. Some call it the quantum field, where nothing and everything exists at the same time as both wave and particle until we, the observers, serve to collapse the wave function and measure or fix reality into position. Until then, all is in a state of superposition. The superconscious is the superpositioned mind.

Where the other levels of consciousness are closely tied into our physical nature, the superconscious goes beyond physicality. An interesting analogy for all of this comes from today's obsession with technology. Imagine your own personal computer. That is your conscious, active mind. Your computer is linked to others all over the globe via the global "network" that allows you to converse with folks in other countries in real time and access almost instantaneously anything you want or need. That is the superconscious mind. Your computer runs on selected programs you chose to have installed with time and may have forgotten you did. That is the subconscious mind. Below all of this is the amassed collective of all of the information on all computers all over the world past, present, and future. That is the collective unconscious.

The "higher mind" may or may not exist outside of the body/ brain as a consciousness that interacts with our brains. This is the domain of universal consciousness, which we are all able to tap into for information we need. This mind knows nothing of linear time or the limitations of space, and is often described as "infinite mind." Here, we find the highest levels of knowledge, creativity, spiritual awareness, oneness, wholeness, and connectedness with the All. Like the Bible's Kingdom of Heaven, it is in and through us and all around us. But we don't have to believe in a religious God to experience this open awareness and destruction of ego and separation.

Where the collective unconscious is the deepest part of us, connected to the unconscious minds of everyone else that get their power from symbols and past programming, the superconscious is the highest part of us, connected to all the conscious minds as well as the mind of what created us: Source, God, Kingdom of Heaven, The Zero Point Field. It is a pure field or "grid" of potentiality from which we co-create our manifest reality.

Some psychologists and scholars claim the superconscious and collective unconscious are the same, but in fact they are quite the opposite of each other. The superconscious knows all and allows us to access it by becoming one with a creative source or force. The collective unconscious is the land of hidden symbolic information of humanity through time, yet continuing to drive our behaviors and personalities below the radar and behind the scenes.

Superconsciousness is God Mind. It is transcendent and divine. The collective unconscious is Humanity Mind. It is instinctual and primal. Both are critical to our understanding of who we are.

As powerful and superior as this level of mind may be, we rarely use it. When we do, we are inspired, acting on what we sense is our higher selves or our creative source energy moving through us, speaking to us. Our conscious mind will often keep us distracted from the whisperings of the superconscious, and our subconscious and collective unconscious might even serve as gatekeepers that refuse to let us into the gates of heaven, so to speak. Acting to keep us afraid, in our comfort zones, safe, and curled into a little ball of habit, pattern, and self-sabotage, the other levels of mind will stop at nothing to keep us from experiencing more of the connection with the superconsciousness we seek in order to align ourselves to our purpose here on Earth.

We can use many tools to reach the superconscious and soak up that inspiration and energy, but we first must deal with the deeper parts of ourselves that resist this because we might change—and change is scary. So whereas the superconscious may be the most desirable level of mind to experience, it is still the rock-bottom level of mind that is driving us away from that experience.

That rock-bottom level is the collective unconscious, where we dance the dance of life immersed in universal beliefs, symbols, and ideas that may or may not be our own, may or may not serve us, and may or may not be in our best interest.

Having a visual understanding of how the mind is structured and what each level is responsible for is helpful in realizing what makes us who we are as individuals and as a species. But it doesn't go far enough to show us *why* we are who we are, and how we can make changes to ourselves and our lives that more fully reflect the truth and authenticity of the person we know somewhere deep within we can be. To do that, we have to step back from speaking the language of the conscious mind, which is focused on words, unexamined beliefs, thoughts, goals, and plans, and begin speaking the language of the collective unconscious. Think of it this way: if a diver wants to get the object on the ocean floor, he/she has to go all the way to the bottom. Unless it floats, it is stuck there in the sand and sediment to be pulled out and examined up in the light of day.

To dive that deep, though, we have to learn to speak in symbols, and the most powerful of these are the archetypes. These mysterious and enigmatic symbols run our lives from their domain, or kingdom, and yet most of us have never even met or acknowledged them.

Until now.

[chapter 2]
Archetypes:
The Language of Symbols

Imagine a kitchen filled with the wonderful smells of baking cookies. There are cookies of all shapes, sizes, flavors, and colors. The kitchen is the collective unconscious filled with symbols of delicious goodness. The cookies are the archetypes that take on a specific shape or form, according to the cookie cutter used. The cookie-cutter cookies all look the same, or at the very least look like they came from the same cookie cutter! But the dough, frosting colors, and additional treats may be different from cookie to cookie.

Archetypes are the symbols of the collective unconscious, and they are original models from which all similar items of the same kind are based. Like the cookie-cutter analogy, a given archetype is the same no matter what, but it can have some add-ons that give it a bit of individuality. Like a batch of Christmas tree cookies, many will be green, some brown, a few may have ornaments, some stars at the top, but all of them are the same shape: Christmas trees.

No matter who we are or where we come from, the language the collective unconscious speaks is the same for all of us, with no interpreters necessary. We get symbols, even if the way we talk about them or express them externally varies in accordance to where we originated and what language we speak. They all mean the same thing.

One of the most well-known archetypes is a hero. There can be millions of kinds of heroes, each doing different things that make them heroic. Some can be knights, some warriors, and some cancer survivors and caretakers. But the general "mold" of a hero is the same no matter where you go in the world.

Thus, when we talk about archetypes, we are talking about "tangible abstracts," which may seem counterintuitive as tangibles are rarely if ever abstract. But we are referring to a concrete mold that symbolizes something, and yet that mold can be decorated in a million different ways.

Before humans could communicate with words, we did so with images, whether painted or carved into rocks, walls, sides of caves, on pottery, or in the dirt. Images symbolized what we wanted to say and express by compacting a description into one form, one glyph, picture, or image. Thus, symbols were the first means of representing an object, idea, or situation into enough data for someone else to understand, and often the understanding occurred in both a very conscious and a subconscious sense. A symbol is nothing more than a visual image that represents both an idea and a deeper universal truth, and because of that, symbols became the language of the subconscious. With often multiple meanings, they require a deeper interpretation, one often based upon sociological, cultural, and personal experiences. Thus, the symbol for something in one country could represent something else entirely in another.

Universal symbols, such as archetypes, go even deeper, because everyone understands their meaning, no matter the social, cultural, racial, or any other differences that may be present on the surface. It doesn't matter where the interpreter is from or what race or gender they are. Universal symbols speak to the deepest parts of us, the parts that are connected to a greater whole where all is one and one is all. In his book with Joseph Campbell, *Philosophies of India*, Heinrich Robert Zimmer, an expert in Indian mythology and historian of South Asian art, states that symbols mirror a transcendent reality whether they be in the form of an object, a custom, a tradition, ritual, or image: "Through all of these a transcendent reality is mirrored. They are so many metaphors reflecting and implying something that, though thus variously expressed, is ineffable, though thus rendered multiform, remains inscrutable. Symbols hold the mind to truth but are not themselves the truth, hence it is delusory to borrow them. Each civilization, every age, must bring forth its own."[1]

But Carl Jung differed in his definition of symbols. Whereas others proposed that a symbol stood for something known, Jung believed symbols stood for something that is unknown, not clear, and not easily discernible or describable. To Jung, the meaning was profound and something only understood by that unknowable part of our minds—the collective unconscious. Experiences that could not be reduced to simple words, such as religious rapture, the depths of love or despair, or the throes of passion or terror, might be better explained with something that reached beyond the surface of the mind to where we all share the same "field of experience," or information, even those we ourselves have not encountered.

Tabula Rasa vs.
Collective Unconscious

One of the many differences Jung had with Freud was the belief about the original state of the mind at birth. Freud sided with the theory of "tabula rasa" or "blank slate" mind, which was popularized by John Locke in his "Essay on Human Understanding" in the late 17th century. Locke, an English philosopher and physician who is widely regarded as a highly influential Enlightenment thinker, was instrumental in the development of liberal theory and political philosophy, as well as in defining both consciousness and empiricism. Locke's "theory of mind" put forward some of the most insightful concepts on identity, self, self-conscious awareness, and the idea that the mind, upon birth, was a blank slate, born without any inherent or innate concepts or ideas. He used the expression "white paper" to describe this mind and posited that the mind after birth processed experiences and ideas solely based upon sensory input.[2]

Earlier, philosophers such as Descartes had suggested that there were indeed innate ideas placed into the mind at birth by God. This was called "continental rationalism." Thomas Aquinas was one of the earliest philosophers to posit the tabula rasa theory as far back as the 13th century, but the earliest mention goes back to the writings of Aristotle and his *De Anima* or *On the Soul*, where he wrote of the "unscribed tablet."[3] Later, Locke added his own spin to the theory of the original mind as blank, and that data was added after birth. Individuals were free to be who they were and make their own choices and have their own beliefs, but their basic identity as a human being was inalterable.

Sigmund Freud utilized the tabula rasa concept in his own psychoanalysis as well. Freud believed that one's personality traits as being formed by family dynamics such as the Oedipus Complex, as well as one's upbringing, with minimal influences based on genetics.

Jung, in contrast, did not accept the "tabula rasa" or white paper explanation of the mind and, instead, proposed that there was a part of each human that, from the moment of birth, contained universal understandings and symbolic wisdom, archetypal in nature, called the collective unconscious. He called these "primordial images" before they became labeled as "archetypes" and were something humans were born with, already tapped into the grid or field of the universal collective, along with every other human being. We were therefore not born a clean slate, but one with invisible writing already written upon our psyches. The archetypes of the collective unconscious seek actualization through the individuation, or balance between the conscious and unconscious, of each person's environment and experiences within that environment, often leading to complexes and predispositions of the psyche and personality.

The end goal was the transformation of the archetype that represented the totality of the psyche: the self.

Ultimately it is up to us, though, to correctly interpret the meaning of symbols, and this has been the bane of those who choose to study ancient texts, imagery, glyphs, art, architecture, and even stories and myths. When it comes to psychoanalysis and knowing thyself, the correct or incorrect interpretation of the archetypes at play in our own lives can make the difference between a successful, happy life and one of misery and defeat (more on that later).

When we look at symbols, especially those that have some importance to us, we do so through the lens of not only external influences, but also who we have come to believe we are as human beings and individuals. One man's pagan symbol is another man's religious symbol. A phrase in a myth might suggest one thing to one person and something else entirely to another. We get into trouble trying to interpret our lives through symbols when we attempt to do so from a more surface level because our differences get in the way.

To work with universal symbols such as archetypes, we must dive as deep as we can into the ocean itself, where we all swim. Here, a fish is a fish to all involved, even if we might call it a different name on the surface. Just acknowledging symbols isn't enough. We might only see what we want to see and not what we need to see. This is why truths, such as those archetypes represent, are often hidden to our conscious minds for fear of overanalysis, misinterpretation, and misidentification. They are hidden in plain sight, though, and have been throughout the history of human development.

Symbols in Stories

An examination of myth, legend, and folktales often reveal just how influenced we are by symbolic entities, often archetypal in nature. Even though we know these stories have a fictional foundation, a part of us senses the deeper truth buried within the tall tale. This also applies to religious stories that appear in our most sacred texts. In fact, Carl Jung believed that contact with archetypes led to the development of both myth and religion, and were one of two ways that information is actually transmitted between people (the other being genetically). The long survival rate of myths, legends, folklore, and fairy tales can attest to the power of symbolic communication.

How old are archetypes and symbols then? Most likely they are as old as humanity itself, and links to them no doubt abound in our history. In a recent article for Ancient-Origins.net, titled "Research Decodes Ancient Celtic Astronomy Symbols and Links Them to Jungian Archetypes," Celtic artifacts were examined and shown to have strong similarities to some of the most basic archetypal symbols, such as the use of X patterns and the sun. X pattern symbols going back as far as 400 BC were found on coins and ceremonial armbands, but also, intriguingly, at ritual places such as Stonehenge and Newgrange. The sun, revered as the giver of life by the ancient Celts, was, according to Dr. Miranda J. Green in *Dictionary of Celtic Myth and Legend*, found on objects of every kind because of its importance as a healing and creative/generative power. It has now been associated with specific X patterns such as four-spoked wheels and repousse crosses. Some of this same symbolism was etched in the great henge monuments themselves.[4,5]

Sacred Geometry

The use of sacred geometry in ancient times attests to the powerful belief that symbols have influence and link directly to greater forces. The idea that "as above, so below" was prevalent when it came to art, architecture, and many other aspects of life, and that what we made, created, built, constructed, and acted on Earth was mirrored in the heavens or vice versa.

Sacred geometry used basic geometrics and mathematical ratios, harmonics and proportion, resonance and vibration, and numeric sequences as the foundation for many sacred structures. The use of such sacred measurements transcended culture, race, and even distance, and seemed to not only emanate from, but resonate with, the collective unconscious of humanity, becoming a foundation for building sacred structures such as temples, mosques, megaliths, monuments, and churches; sacred spaces such as altars, temenoi, and tabernacles; meeting places such as sacred groves, village greens, and holy wells; and the creation of religious art, iconography, and using "divine" proportions. Sacred geometry in art speaks to the deepest parts of the subconscious, as in mandalas, labyrinths, medicine wheels, mazes, and other highly patterned objects including crop circles (man-made or otherwise!).

The concept of sacred geometry harkens back to the beliefs of Plato, who ascribed the "geometrization" of the universe to God. Modern quantum physicists and scientists agree that the basic language of the universe is numbers and mathematical ratios, even going so far as to suggest that when we one day communicate with aliens, it will be using math and not language itself. By observing nature and the laws that govern it, which were mathematical, ancient philosophers understood that what appeared to govern life on Earth was also at play in the cosmic sense and, as Leonardo da Vinci drew in his famous "Vitruvian Man," in our own bodies as well. Number sequences and ratios appear everywhere, from the logarithmic growth spirals of a Nautilus shell or a sunflower's petals to the planetary spacing of our own solar system, to the shape of galaxies millions of light years away, and they speak of a deeper knowledge that speaks to the soul via dimensions, proportions, and measurements that strike a certain aesthetic we often cannot explain using regular words and descriptions.

One might almost posit that sacred geometry is the visual representation of archetypal symbols that describe nature and our place in it. By taking the language of the universe itself and giving it a sacredness of symbolic interpretation, we see just how microcosm and macrocosm mirror each other and create something our subconscious minds resonate with.

Motifs

In myths and other forms of storytelling these symbols were called "motifs" and have been called the categories of the imagination. A widely recognized motif is the hero's journey, as detailed in Joseph Campbell's works in comparative mythology such as the *Power of Myth* series and *The Hero with a Thousand Faces*. Another is the great flood, stories of which are found in global myths, origin stories, religious texts, and folklore, from the *Epic of Gilgamesh* to the Old Testament's Noah and his ark. Motifs can also show up in artistic representations that are similar in appearance despite cultural and geographic differences and in mythological figures that have different names, yet are the same personas/deities.

Jung himself used the word "idea" to often describe archetypes. This may be traced back to the use of the term by St. Augustine in *De deversis quaestionibus*, where he writes of the "ideas which are not yet formed…which are contained in the divine intelligence," but that these ideas are also prototypes. For example, the reference to God as "to archetypon phos" in the 3rd century *Corpus Hermeticum* is said to suggest that God, at least in an archetypal sense, is a prototype of light itself.[6] Thus, each archetype may in fact be the original form of what it represents, a "sample" or "example," indeed even a blueprint, of something real and tangible, just as a prototype of a plane or invention is a sample/example/blueprint of the plane or invention that evolves from it.

Dreams

One of the most powerful places Jung found the presence of archetypes lurking was in dreams and he wrote about it extensively. His approach differed from Freud's who saw lesser importance in the symbolism of vivid dreams and visions. Jung recorded his dreams, as well as his fantasies and visions, in detail and felt strongly that in the dream state, archetypes spoke to the psyche. The collective unconscious to Jung was a treasure trove of information and often it emerged in the dream state as symbols, recurring motifs, and powerful themes and messages that linked the imagination directly into the collective unconscious and the language of archetypes. And what better time to allow the world of symbol and depth to emerge than when the conscious mind is fast asleep and the analytical brain is shut down for the night?

Think about dreams. Our conscious minds rarely grasp their bizarre nature or meaning, but on a subconscious or unconscious level we get what they are working on, working out, or trying to tell us. Dream symbolism is a huge field of study done mainly by those interested in psychology and psychoanalysis, but also those who are interested in the metaphysical and spiritual worlds. Identifying and working with dream imagery can help us get a better understanding of what obstacles and challenges we face, what we are denying and resisting, and what past experiences and memories are still at play in our present.

Freud and Jung were pioneers in the use of dreams and dream analysis to explore the depths of the unconscious mind, but where they differed was in the interpretation. Freud believed that dreams and the symbolism found therein were more about repressed desires, especially sexual, and were a mask of the true feelings a person was trying to keep below the surface. In dreams, the things we dared not speak of or think about had their freedom of expression, and that expression occurred as symbols to be understood by the sub-conscious mind.

To Jung, dreams were much more. Jung felt that dreams were a guide or manual of sorts to help understand the conscious and waking state. Dreams were thick with solutions to problems that a person might not be able to access in the waking state, and they were filled with the very archetypes active in the person's own psyche. By analyzing the dream symbols and the overall visions themselves, Jung believed one could truly find the keys to the doors of wholeness, growth, and evolution of consciousness, both on a personal and collective level.

Perhaps a better way to differentiate Freud and Jung and their belief in the power of dreams would be to say Freud examined dreams from their objective level and Jung from the subjective. Freud looked for ways dreams related to the real-life experiences of the individual, and Jung approached them from the symbolic, psychological aspect of personal transformation and what was needed to achieve it, or being oppressed to prevent it. Freud's analysis was more retrospective, looking at the influence of past events on the present. Jung, on the other hand, was prospective, looking at how dreams could be used to create a balance between the ego and the unconscious for future transformation. Jung looked at various parts of dreams as being out of the range of conscious understanding, and without any associated experience that a person might reference them back to. This is because the aspects of a dream were meant to be understood symbolically by the subconscious and unconscious minds.

An example of this might be a dream of your mother. Freud might interpret that dream as some repressed expression you have toward your own mother that you may or may not be aware of. Jung would instead look at the mother in the dream as a representation of the archetypal feminine aspect of the psyche, known as the "anima." The mother in a dream can mean so much more than the woman who gave birth to you!

Jung even went a few steps further with dream analysis. He also applied theories of "compensation" and "amplification" to the symbols. Compensation looked at dreams as a means of counterbalancing, or compensating for, strong psychological tendencies that manifested in a person's attitudes, behaviors, and beliefs. Compensation sought to correct those imbalances and bring about more harmony and wholeness. Amplification was the idea that images and symbols from our dreams could be amplified or expanded upon via associations from myths, religion, folklore, and cultural influences.[7]

The dream state is rich with symbols that speak to each of us on both a personal and a collective level. In dreams, we navigate the depths of our own psyches, yet also share a landscape known to all, a universal level of nonwaking reality where we can all fly, shape shift, see through walls, ride atop of dragons, and do other things we cannot do when we are awake. Each person knows, on a subconscious level, what the things he or she dreams about mean in reference to his or her own psyche and personal development. And, as in our waking state, the universal symbolism and common motifs help us understand on a greater and deeper scale what it means to be a human being.

Sacred Objects

Even objects can be archetypes. Those objects that hold deep meaning for larger segments of the world take on a universal nature. One that comes to mind is the Holy Grail of the King Arthur legends, which is also linked to the chalice from which Christ drank at the Last Supper. This singular item has taken on a symbolic meaning that is understood by even those who are not Christian or do not know of the King Arthur connection, because the words "Holy Grail" have become a part of our language to describe something that is highly sought after, desired, or of great worth.

The Holy Bible is archetypal of a religion that has profoundly changed history. The cross itself is a symbol that needs no explanation, for it represents the suffering of the Christ figure in Christianity. The Swastika, although it originated as a pagan flag, now strikes horror into the soul as a symbol of death, violence, and incredible oppression of human life. Even the Batman symbol is recognizable the world over as signifying something heroic, just as the outline of a heart signifies love no matter who we are or where we go.

Any object that holds a deeper meaning on a more universal scale can be said to have archetypal qualities, even if it does not match the description of a Jungian archetype.

Places, too, can be archetypal. Think of the standing stones of Stonehenge that represent a mysterious meeting place of the Druids; they evoke a universal quality of otherworldliness as with the massive standing rock heads of Easter Island. The Bermuda Triangle has entered the pop culture lexicon of an archetypal location where unusual, even paranormal things, occur—a place to be avoided at all costs. Las Vegas represents an archetype of hedonism, decadence, and forbidden desires, as if the city were herself an actual temptress or goddess. Hollywood and its iconic sign above the hills overlooking the city of Los Angeles has become the symbol of fame and fortune.

In the next chapter we begin to look at actual archetypes, major and minor, personal and collective, and what they mean. To understand their influence in our lives, and how we can change them, we must first name them.

[chapter 3]

Archetypes and
Their Meanings

When it comes to archetypes, there are the originals that Jung worked with in his psychoanalysis, and there are a host of others that have been added on by those who have furthered Jung's work and taken on the subject themselves. For purposes of this book, and in the spirit of not complicating the process of understanding and using these symbols to transform one's life, we won't list every single archetype put forth by every John and Jane Doe out there. Suffice it to say, there truly are only a limited number of them that are actively influencing our psyches. Though we might name them differently, they still represent the same foundational role.

When looking at the experiences of men and women in a collective sense, Jung came up with "the big four" that he most utilized in his work. These four serve as the most critical to understand any others that came after them, and he himself had quite a list. Other scholars have added their own interpretations and insights onto these archetypes.

PERSONA: We all wear masks to give a particular impression to the world around us. The persona is the mask we put on to present ourselves to others and our environments. The persona is our public role, the image we want to be seen and known as, and the way we choose to conform and fit in with society. The persona is not the real self, but a self we choose to portray for whatever ends and means are needed. Imagine someone attending a masquerade ball. He wants to hide his real identity and chooses a mask, elaborate or simple, to allow him to move in the world without revealing who he truly is.

The persona can be a professional title, a family role, or our place in the community at large. It is used to keep our private life hidden, and to allow us to be a part of the greater social order.

ANIMA/ANIMUS: We each have a mirror image of our sexual gender that takes on the characteristics of the opposite sex and acts unconsciously within the psyche. The anima is the female self that manifests in males, and the animus is the male side that manifests in females. So a woman's psyche will contain aspects of the male, or animus, and the man's psyche will contain aspects of the female, or anima. The anima is the symbol of the feminine aspects of a man, and the animus, the masculine aspects in each woman. The anima may manifest emotionally and be a force of life and nature. The animus may be logical, rational, and analytical.

SHADOW: This is the primal, animal side to us. It is Freud's "id." The shadow is the darker nature of our psyche, often survival-based and capable of both creative and destructive powers. It is our shadow self, the side to us we often don't want to acknowledge, and the realm of the personal unconscious. This is our repressed side and often takes on a negative connotation. It is also the inferior or undeveloped aspects of our personality, and includes animal tendencies that Jung believed were inherited from pre-human ancestors. The shadow can manifest individually, but also collectively in the world as dark, even demonic, activity.

SELF: This is the idealized, unified whole of our psyche that balances the shadow and the self, the anima and the animus. This is the real person actualized and was, to Jung, the ultimate goal of a human being and the greatest state of personal and spiritual achievement. The self is the unity of the personality as a whole, an entirety. It is the most important of all archetypes and the one to aspire to. Human examples of the mastery of self include the Christ and the Buddha and sometimes take on the image of pairs—a child and parent, king and queen, god and goddess.

Other important archetypes in the Jungian hierarchy include:

The Great Mother and the Maiden (her counterpart): Because we were all infants once, we all have as a part of our psyche a mother, who starts out as a young maiden, and represents such qualities as caretaker, guide, nurturer, protector, and giver of life. Even surrogate mothers, adoptive mothers, and other relatives who take on a mothering role can display the qualities required because all cultures understand what makes someone a mother. Even a father can be a mother! However, most mother symbolism is feminine and involves such symbols as the moon in all its fullest phase, deep water and the ocean to represent the waters of the womb, chalices and vessels to represent the receptivity of the womb, and the Earth itself. After all, we do call it Mother Earth. A person's relationship with his or her mother is the most critical to early development and often leads to behaviors and character traits that stay embedded in subconscious programming for life unless addressed and, if needed, changed. In some literature such as fairy tales, a wicked or abusive stepmother represents the darker aspects of the mother.

The maiden aspect can represent feminine purity, or she can be pregnant with newfound life. She is usually representative of beauty and a spiritual quality, although she may have an opposing principle in the wicked young witch in training or the child devourer of some Eastern myths. The maiden is still a sexual being, although even when she becomes the mother, she is still the giver of life and can have a powerful, if often suppressed, sexuality. Perhaps we can go one step further and say that the crone is the grandmother aspect that completes the "maiden-mother-crone" triad found in many pagan and earth-based traditions.

The Child: This archetype may not truly be a child, but an original or an individual at his or her most childlike before being changed and formed by society. The child may also be represented by a dwarf, elf, or even an animal, and is meant to bring the individual back to the roots when he/she has strayed too far toward an imbalance. The child can also represent the urge felt to achieve a state of self-realization.

The Hero: Male or female, the hero represents the aspect that accepts the challenge of the journey to the self, to wholeness, and to destiny. Part sage, warrior, innocent, superhero, and courageous lionhearted soul, the hero within is the part of us that is good and true and willing to go through the trials of growth and transformation, even as it will lead us into the darkness of the abyss and bring us into contact with our own demons, monsters, and beasts. The life of a human is a hero's journey, a concept made popular by comparative mythologist Joseph Campbell. The hero seeks justice, harmony, and balance in the world, and within his or her self.

The Wise Old Man/Woman: This spirit can be a sage, priest, priestess, authority figure, mentor, or even a king or queen that has incredible insight, wisdom, and morality. The wise old man is a grandfatherly figure that can be both protective and reactive, warn of future dangers, be watchful and, of course, wise. He can be cranky and cantankerous as well as kind and gentle, much like any grandfather might be! The wise old woman likewise is a grandmotherly figure, wise and understanding, and ready to impart feminine wisdom to the youngsters who seek her out.

Archetypes in literature often mirror those of Jungian psychology, but add more symbolic characters found in the most universally entertaining books, films, and television shows. This is no mistake, for often writers and other creators are aware of the use of archetypes in their work, even if they do it subconsciously. The act of creating is itself about bringing the conscious and the subconscious, even the collective unconscious, into a piece of work that appeals to an audience on a deeper, grander scale, one they may not even be able to identify. The best and most lasting forms of expression don't have to speak to us on a conscious level, because our collective souls get what they are trying to convey in art, words, music, images, stories, and more.

There are many additional archetypes that show up not just in our pop culture, but in work being done by therapists, healers, and psychologists who seek to affect change from within to help bring about external changes (more on that later). Aside from Jungian psychology, an archetype can be simply a statement/pattern of behavior or a prototype that is emulated or copied by other statements/patterns of behavior. Thus the archetypes discussed next are examples of root symbols that are both universal and identifiable to cultures around the globe, but also operate on a deeper, collective unconscious level as much as they do a conscious and obvious one. For example, the white flag is known to mean "surrender" by the world's armies, but on a more personal level, it can signify a "giving in and giving up" of a bad habit, behavioral pattern, even an addiction to someone or something.

As we progress as human beings and evolve our conscious awareness, and perhaps even our links to the collective unconscious, no doubt some archetypes will be considered archaic and replaced with new, more applicable ones. For example, yesterday's misfit might be today's geek/nerd. The devil of the past might be the political leader of tomorrow. And as we take on new professions, careers, and vocations, we may come to associate ourselves with new roles that are entrenched in symbolism and universal understanding. Even our cultural behaviors will add to the list. Could "cougar" be an archetype of an attractive older woman who likes younger men? Might "jock" be considered an archetype that anyone in any country would find identifiable? We all have the "black sheep" in the family who isn't invited to summer picnics! Though the actual words might be different in each language, no doubt what they represent is common for all of us. Take a look at the strange words that go viral in today's world of social networking; they just might be the archetypes of our time when someone in the future looks back and wonders, "Who were they?"

Jung's primordial images aside, we are now more evolved and no doubt are operating my newer, more modern universal archetypes that have been added to or layered upon the more primitive ones. This book makes no attempt to change or add more Jungian archetypes, but to add those that represent the new and more expansive views we have of ourselves, our species, and the universe in general.

The following list is compiled from a variety of sources, but also comes from the author's own experiences writing and researching symbols and symbolism, work in the recovery field, and being a creative writer who uses archetypes in fiction and film writing. It is by no means exhaustive. These are the symbols by which we live our lives and are the universal foundations of our identities we share the world over—for better and for worse.

Alpha: Refers to the "alpha dog" and can apply to a male or female. This is a take-charge individual, forceful, and usually the leader of the pack. In lingo, he/she is the "big dog."

Angel: Good and pure, yet can also be a dark angel that is sinful, but seeks moral rehabilitation. Winged or human, someone who lifts, carries, helps, and saves others. Guardian angels are included here, whether of the heavenly or human kind.

Anti-Hero: An older archetype of a hero, male or female, that does not embody the normal traits of a hero such as moralism, idealism, and even courage, and in fact does the heroic thing mainly for self-satisfaction or some ego-centric need. The anti-hero was a popular character in classical Greek tragedies, Roman dramas, Renaissance literature, and shows up in a lot of current pop culture. Roland Deschain of Stephen King's *Dark Tower* series comes to mind, as does *The Dark Knight*.

Artist: A creator of art and beauty; someone who sees the artistic and creative side of things. Expressive of the aesthetic value and characteristics of a person, place, or object. This is a painter of reality and of the imagination.

Beast: A monster, but more human than the more literal monster archetype. The beast could be someone like Hitler, a serial killer, or even a part of ourselves we are terrified of because of its capability for violence. It can also represent our primitive nature and the primitive origins of humanity. The beast can also be a positive and beneficial creature met along the hero's journey, and a part of us that is perhaps big in scope, a little out of our control, but not harmful if befriended. It can also be the ugly side of us we sometimes express that hides an inner vulnerability, such as in the fairy tale, "Beauty and the Beast."

Betrayer: Often found in both romance and politics, the betrayer is one who takes trust and destroys it. A traitor or a heartbreaker, a betrayer can often be the part of us that betrays our goals and dreams and sabotages our happiness.

Boss: The boss can represent the symbol of a bossy employer, who orders his or her employees around, but also of a beneficent and caring supervisor. It can also apply to someone who has mastered a level of experience and expertise at something, such as Bruce Springsteen, the rocker known as "The Boss."

Caretaker: A caretaker is a human angel and nurturer, male or female, who can take on the role of looking after another human being, an animal, an object, and even a special and sacred location, such as a church or graveyard. A caretaker is often protective, loyal, and giving to the point of almost being a martyr. Selfless and empathic, virtuous and true, caretakers can also be incredibly strong and resilient.

Chosen One: This can apply to a person who is chosen by a religious tradition, a particular culture, or perhaps a myth such as the dangerous adventure in which only he or she can succeed at. This archetype can also apply to a group of people, such as the Jews, or even the Aryans, whom Adolf Hitler and his followers revered as the archetype of a chosen and pure race. In the book *Black Sun*, author and researcher Nicholas Goodrick-Clarke writes of how Carl Jung described Hitler with the following words: "Hitler was possessed by the archetype of the collective Aryan unconscious and could not help obeying the commands of an inner voice."[1] This implies that there are archetypes that represent collective groups which people identify with, giving those groups a spiritual, almost divine nature that inspires reverence, even if the goals of the group are evil.

Jung felt Hitler was the personification of this archetype and possessed of the traits and characteristics of the Aryan race that inspired his quest for power and conquest.

Creator: A creator archetype can be both like a god or creative source of the universe, or someone that creates. Similar to the artist, a creator can have a vivid and generative imagination and give birth in a sense to new ideas, concepts, and things. The writer, the poet, the singer, and the innovator are all creative archetypes.

Damsel in Distress: Think of old Western movies where the pretty woman waited to be rescued from the rapscallion bad guy by some good-looking hero—or even anti-hero! This archetype can be both a strong woman in real need of help, or imply a weak and conniving woman who purposely waits for a man to rescue her. Yes, there can be males in distress as well! But there might be a better word for that kind of a man, such as "kept."

Desperado: Usually a male, but can be a female who is broken and alone, and often because of their own fear and avoidance of others. A desperado is running from something, perhaps a shady past, or most likely their own shadow and pain. He/she is never a happy figure until something happens to cause him or her to stop, reassess their loner status and settle down, or right a wrong and find justice after all.

Destroyer: The opposite of a creator, someone who destroys things, whether it be other people, objects, or situations. This is a destructive soul, but not necessarily evil. A drug addict or alcoholic who destroys his or her happy home or marriage can qualify here.

Devil: A popular archetype that can represent the actual Devil himself, or the devilish aspects in a human being. The devil goes by many names including Satan, Lucifer, Beelzebub, Old Nick, and the Prince of Darkness, but always represents the opposite of light, goodness, morality, virtue, and peacefulness. Male or female, the devil archetype is the shadow self and the dark side combined, and can also be the expression of evil, violence, and destruction in an otherwise good heart. The devil can also represent free will and the ability to choose that which is not good or for the benefit of others. Often, he is the combination of our own inner demons in manifest form, and can even be the death we so fear.

The devil can also be our inner repressed sexual urges and desires, especially those that might be considered taboo. It is said that in order to achieve wholeness and enlightenment, we must first "meet and beat the Devil within." This constant internal struggle can itself be the devil in archetypal form.

Dictator: Arrogant ruler, control freak. He/she must have things done his/her way, is bossy, demanding, and often lacking in empathy or compassion for others' points of view.

Diplomat: A peacemaker and collaborator skilled in bringing opposing ideas, viewpoints, and sides together; a go-between who is good at seeing the positive; a mediator and interloper.

Diva: Arrogant, show off, conceited, and condescending, this is a modern archetype for our age of social networking fame.

Doppelganger: A literary archetype that identifies the duplicate or shadow/evil part of the personality. Think of *Dr. Jekyll and Mr. Hyde*.

Explorer: The adventurer in all of us; the one who explores and is curious to seek out a quest or adventure; and the part of us that wants to ask questions and find answers, and possibly leave the comfort of the shore for the high seas. The explorer is about the part of us that wants freedom and to discover who we are by exploring the world around us. The explorer is the wanderer within, and the pilgrim on pilgrimage.

Father: An authority figure, often one that is harsh and to be feared. This is the "father figure" and fatherly aspect of the personality, but can also be supportive, proud, and a mentor.

Femme Fatale: Sexual and seductive, the femme fatale can be anything from a woman who knows what she wants and how to get it, to a dangerously seductive siren who uses her sexuality to her advantage, even if it harms others. In pop culture, the femme fatale is often a jealous rival, a mistress, a powerful business adversary, and even a manipulative murderess.

Fool: The fool is confused and often wandering aimlessly, without direction. We all have a fool within us that does stupid, foolish things, and makes poor choices. We have been a "fool for love" many times.

Free Spirit: The part of us that does not like rules and is uninhibited; the free and unlimited aspect of self and humanity; and the joyful and spirited part of us that does not like to be constricted in any way.

Geek/Nerd: A more modern archetype in pop culture that often goes hand in hand with the outcast, genius, and misfit. Different and possibly isolated, it can be the part of our nature that we are embarrassed to display in general, but proud of when with like-minded souls.

Genius: The brilliant one, the problem solver, and the intellectually powerful part of who we are. This is the untapped brilliance and potential we all have deep within.

Girl/Boy Next Door: A wonderful archetype in modern pop culture that represents wholeness and wholesomeness. This is the part of the psyche that seeks to be normal and accepted and doesn't wish to stand out.

God: The powerful deity. This archetype represents our powerful, creative, and prideful nature where we think we are divine. It can be negative, as in believing oneself to be God and controlling others. It is masculine energy and associated with the male ego, but also with the human as divinity. It can also be the perfection of self.

Goddess: The same as God, but feminine. She is the great Mother, or Mother Earth, but also the great Mother that exists in all women. The sexual ideal, beautiful even in her flaws, she is a woman in touch with her own power to create and destroy.

Gypsy: A symbol most often used in modern times for someone's free-spirited, bohemian nature. Unique and somewhat exotic, it represents our innate desire to be totally authentic and living from spirit.

Healer: An individual or collective healer such as a medicine man or woman, witch doctor, physician, or just someone who has the ability to heal others of emotional, spiritual, and physical pain.

Henchman: The follower aspect of the psyche that takes orders and carries them out without moral questioning. They are the underlings working for a bad boss. Often this is the part of us that is detached from feeling, emotion, and empathy and does what we are told.

Hermaphrodite: The inner diplomat that joins the male and female opposites.

Initiate: The beginner on a hero's journey of discovery. He/she is also the newly enlightened or wizened one.

Innocent: The pure, childlike, untainted aspect not yet made cynical or sinful. The innocent within is often naïve and a bit of a dreamer, but can also be a saint without mistake or sin.

Jester: The performer in us. Not a fool, but a "court performer" who plays a role to impress those of higher authority. This can also be the part of us that uses humor as a tool or weapon. It's the frivolous aspect of the self that likes to play and live in the moment. To the extreme, the jester can be a time-waster and distracter from goals.

Judge: The part of us that judges ourselves, others, and conditions and situations. The judge is often a very harsh taskmaster, with a narrow-minded and even black and white view of right and wrong.

Justice: The equalizer who seeks justice and fairness. The justice archetype can be represented by a judge or by the scales of justice. It represents balance and harmony within or the lack thereof.

Killer: The violent and destructive part of us capable of taking another's life. It is the destroyer. It can also represent the part of us that is unrelenting and driven, as in the business world. "She was a killer when it came to closing the deal." It is brutal and compassionless.

King: The royal, regal leader, either for good or for evil, as with any real king.

Leader: The part of us driven to lead others and ourselves, especially when confronted with challenges.

Loner/Lone Wolf: Like the misfit or outcast, the loner can choose to be alone or be cast out by society in general. It is the part of us that desires solitude and self-reliance, and the part of us that shuns society and other human beings.

Lover: The romantic and empathic, compassionate aspect. This archetype represents the one who chooses love over hate, peace over violence. It is the nurturing, caring, and expansive aspect of heart and spirit. It's also chivalrous and sensual.

Magician: One who can transform and possesses magical abilities and knowledge. This is the visionary and manifester who can make dreams real. This part of ourselves is in tune with the laws of nature and the universe, and knows how to use them for good or evil intentions. The magician is an inventor, creator, and catalyst.

Martyr: The part of us that is self-sacrificing to a fault, giving too much and suffering for others. The inner martyr can be an extreme of other-directed care at the total expense of self-care. It's the part of us that sacrifices our happiness, goals, and dreams and suffers for it.

Mentor: The protector of the initiate and innocent. The mentor is a wiser, often older teacher and purveyor of wisdom. It is the "higher self" that we can tap into for wisdom, guidance, and advice. It's the part of our psyche that wants to protect and guide the innocence we see in ourselves and in others.

Messenger: The carriers and catalysts of a message important to humanity, such as Christ, the Buddha, and Hermes/Mercury. The messenger is often as important as the message, especially when combined with the messiah archetype!

Messiah: Can also be the chosen one. Someone looked upon as a leader of humanity, a savior who will rescue us from chaos, sin, and destruction, and fix the world. In our own psyches, the messiah is the part of ourselves that can save us from our own attempts to self-destruct and perhaps save others who seek our help.

Monster: Similar to the beast, a violent and dark side that can be incredibly destructive. In pop culture, it can be terrible and horrific as in *Godzilla*, or a companion to a misfit or lonely child that needs a friend.

Nightmare Creature: This refers to the horrible entities of our nightmares. They are the demons and monsters that haunt our dreams, yet bear gifts to the psyche because they expose deep-rooted fears and concerns that have not been dealt with.

Orphan: The abandoned one within. This is the parentless child, lost and alone, on his or her own journey. It is the part of us that must "go it alone" and undergo certain challenges to grow up into our adult selves.

Outcast/Misfit: The uncelebrated part of our persona we often hide. It's the inner freak that does not fit in, but also the "unchosen one" that we identify ourselves with. The outcast is more bold and rebellious, choosing to not fit in and go against the grain. The misfit may feel cast out involuntarily and wants to fit in, but doesn't.

Outlaw: The lawbreaker and nonconformist within, and within society. The one who takes what he/she wants without working for it. He or she obeys no laws or rules and causes trouble for the rest of society and the self.

Poser: The one who presents a mask to the world and to the self. It's the faker, the fraud, and the part of us that pretends to be more. It is the exaggerator and embellisher, the masked man or woman who hides the truth.

Prince/Princess: Often portrayed as haughty and entitled, the "little kings and queens" that demand the best, whether they've earned it or not. It's our inner spoiled child, but can also be honorable and kind, chivalrous and virtuous.

Pupil: The student and learner. This is the one who seeks advice and knowledge. It's the aspect that always strives to know more and is a seeker of wisdom.

Queen: The partner or female aspect of the king. She is royal, honorable, and worthy of worship if positive. The negative aspect can be controlling, bossy, mean, and even totally lacking in compassion.

Rebel: The defiant one within. These are the defiant and rebellious members of the collective, who challenge the rules and powers of authority figures. It's the part of us that breaks the rules and turns away from conformity. It is the revolutionary and iconoclast.

Both James Dean and Luke Skywalker can be considered rebels in pop culture.

Ruler: The part of the self that wants to rule and control all other parts or aspects. It's the one that wants control the masses; it is the inner bossy control freak or aristocrat and the "manager of the mind."

Sage: The wise truth-knower and the expert scholar within. The sage is the philosopher and thinker and the one that seeks out knowledge to share. The goal of the sage is to know truth and live by it and from it.

Scapegoat: The one that suffers because of the sins and shortcomings of others. This is the aspect within us that suffers our bad choices, negative thinking, and destructive behaviors.

Side Kick: The alter-ego or even helper to achieving the self's goals and desires. It can be a part of the psyche that supports the self, but never overrides it.

Superman/Superwoman: The overachiever and superhero in all of us. It can benefit us as much as exhaust and destroy us. This is the part of us that wants to fix, do, save, achieve, and handle.

Survivor: The part of the self or collective that survives trauma, obstacles, and challenges. This is the struggler; often seen as negative because of the focus on struggle, as opposed to success. It can also mean the "last man standing."

Teacher: One who helps guide the child and innocent within. This is a higher self that knows the answers to our lower self's questions.

Tempter/Temptress: The distracting, seductive side to the self that keeps us from our journey's goals and from our destinies. This can also be an outside force that makes us deviate from our path and often our morals and values.

Trickster: A troublemaker, mischief-maker, or rascal aspect that taunts and teases us to look deeper, change, and transform. Beneficial to growth, but annoying, as in the persistent, still voice within that urges us to break out of a comfort zone despite our fears, and can trick us into change if we are not willing.

Underling: The follower that takes orders from authority figures without question of right and wrong. This is the stooge, lackey, and worker drone. It is the disempowered part of the self.

Victim: The one who suffers. This is the broken, beaten down aspect of the self. It is the martyr or fool that suffers a bad fate. The victim within can keep us weak, trapped, sick, and unable to improve our lot in life.

Villain: The bad guy or girl within. He/she is the enemy and one who breaks "the law." However, the villain archetype can often be a catalyst for the biggest growth by breaking laws that keep one from happiness and success.

Visionary: The part of us that sees the bigger picture and takes an expansive view of things. It is the creative, generative, inventive, and enlightened part of us that puts forth new ideas, concepts, and understandings.

Warrior: The fighter within that allows us to face challenges with bold courage. It is the lion within, the determined, dedicated aspect that does not give up.

Wizard: The part of us that has power over hidden forces and hidden wisdom, knows of the inner transformation we need, and how to manifest it. It is similar to the sage, but capable of magic as in the ability to transform and transmute, such as the alchemist who turns base metal into gold. Think of Merlin from the King Arthur tales.[2, 3, 4]

Chances are you recognized a variety of these present in your own life and in a part of who you believe yourself to be. But before we look at whether these archetypes are serving or sabotaging you, there are situations, objects, and events that also qualify as archetypes, and some may surprise you.

One of the leading writers and spiritual teachers using archetypes is Caroline Myss, author of *Sacred Contracts: Awakening Your Divine Potential* and *Anatomy of the Spirit*, among other books specifically focused on archetypes and how to work with them. She lists more than 70 archetypes she has identified in working with people, many of which were just listed. They include: the companion, historian, muse, poet, addict, coward, mystic, clown, bully, avenger, hermit, pioneer, predator, scholar, tyrant, zombie, seer, shaman, witch, prostitute, and puppet, among others she has indentified.[5]

The most important thing that separates a symbol from an archetype, though, is the universality of its characteristics and behaviors. So a symbolic figure that is only known in a small town may be important to the collective unconscious of that little town, but it is not an archetype working on the grander collective scale.

Situational Archetypes

Rites of passage and life events can also have an archetypal quality, as well as other situations and circumstances that are shared by populaces all over the world. Though each nation or culture may do these life events a bit differently, the core meaning is often so similar as to not be a coincidence. Burials and weddings come readily to mind, but there are also many rituals surrounding coming of age, too, as well as life phases we all go through no matter who we are or where we live.

Jung believed that situational archetypes were the stages of life that included the birth of babies, death, marriage, any separation from parents (going off to college), initiation events such as a girl's first menses, and the unification of any opposites. We might add to this list dating and courtship, engagement, pregnancy, menopause, the first sexual experience, the first job, and perhaps even midlife crises, because these are symbolic events that occur in more than just one part of the world and have a universal quality to them.

For some cultures, there are "coming of age" rites of passage celebrations and rituals such as the Quinceanera of Mexicans that introduces young women into society with lavish parties and colorful gowns, the bar mitzvahs/bat mitzvahs of the Jewish people, and even the American "sweet sixteen" parties, all of which share common ideals and mark a powerful rite of passage. Other cultures have cotillions and initiations that transition children into early adulthood and prepare them for the coming responsibilities of marriage, jobs, and raising families. In many African countries, young men and women coming of age must go through a number of initiations and rituals before they can be accepted as adults and functioning members of society. Often, the initiate is sent into some type of isolation first, to give him or her the opportunity to gain self-knowledge and get in contact with spirit guides that will be with them for the rest of their lives to guide and direct them.

Each life stage is itself archetypal, with youth giving way to adulthood and then to old age. The transitions from one phase to another are celebrated the world over, as is the final phase or stage, preparing for actual death and the following funeral rites. We also have symbolic events along the way such as puberty, dating, first jobs, marriage, divorce, menopause, midlife crisis, and the golden years.

We will take a more in-depth look at one of the most powerful situational archetypes in a later chapter—the journey. The life of a human being—no matter their race, gender, color, or creed—can be summed up as a journey made up of key points that serve as "landmarks" along the way. The initiation begins the journey, which is usually about confronting inner demons or facing outer obstacles, such as a fall from grace or a struggle between good and evil, and often ends with a fall into the abyss from which the journeyer arises stronger and more powerful than before, armed and equipped with new skills, resources, and knowledge.

Archetypal Functions

Symbols and motifs that reoccur throughout religious texts, myths, origin stories, literature, art, architecture, and all forms of media are also considered archetypes. Carl Jung said in *Man and His Symbols* that "The archetype is a tendency to form such representation of a motif—representations that can vary a great deal in detail without losing their basic pattern." These motifs are what Jung called "an instinctive trend."[6]

Objects

To primitive and even ancient cultures, all the way up to the present, certain objects symbolize more than their apparent and surface explanations and functions. Fire, for example, is an archetypal object that represents cleansing, purification, change, and is also associated with rising from adversity and transformation. But it is also fire.

The sun, moon, stars, and certainly the constellations of astrology have been considered representations of creation, birth, death, love, sex, and war, among other things. Wilfred L. Guerin writes in "Mythological and Archetypal Approaches," in his book *A Handbook of Critical Approaches to Literature*, that common symbols "carry the same or similar meanings for a large portion, if not all, of mankind." He continues on to explain that certain symbols such as "sky father and earth mother, light, blood, up-down and others recur again and again in cultures so remote from one another in time and space that there is no likelihood of any historical influence and casual connection among them."[7]

Deborah Rudd, in "Examples of Archetypes, Literature," lists some of the common objects that take on archetypal qualities:

- Water: Birth, creation, the womb, purification, growth, including things like oceans, seas, rivers, and lakes.
- Sun: Fire, creative energy, cleansing, wisdom, and spiritual vision with the rising sun symbolic of birth, and the setting sun, death.
- Serpent: Energy, libido, evil, sensuality, and corruption.
- Colors with their respective associations such as red (blood); green (fertility); black (chaos); and white (purity).
- Numbers: Examples would be three (the Holy Trinity, Unity); four (seasons, elements, life cycle); and seven (perfection as the union of three and four).[8]

Add to this list the moon and her phases, which hold incredible importance for primitive and pagan cultures, as well as modern-day witches and Wiccans; trees, which represent the levels of mind, as well as the center of the world to many cultures, such as the Norse Yggdrasil, World Tree, and the Kabbalistic Tree of Life; light and dark as the conscious and subconscious; phallic symbols as representative of creation and procreation; the desert as desolation, emptiness, and despair; the garden as paradise, fertility, and growth; the four seasons as spring (rebirth), summer (abundance), autumn (withdrawal), and winter (death), followed by rebirth in the never-ending cycle of life, which itself a strong archetype. Circles represent connectedness and the infinite; pyramids symbolize the phallus, but also the perfection of the triangle, a revered and sacred geometric form. A bull is a masculine force; a deer a feminine and delicate force; and an eagle or wolf most always symbolize honor and nobility.

Religions of the world share them as well, with common concepts of heaven and hell, good vs. evil, and demons and angels. Other symbolic archetypes include wandering in the desert; the underworld; the crossroads and destiny; the castle as a stronghold; the threshold or edge; supernatural interventions (good and bad); fog and storms; towers; forests; lakes; and a host of others. The tower, for example, can represent to many cultures the act of isolation, whether voluntary or imposed. The magic weapon is the object someone finds and uses on a quest to help complete a challenge or adventure. A chalice represents being receptive to knowledge or even the act of sexual intercourse when accompanied by the blade.

Freud had his own archetypes, which had a more sexual bent. Phallic symbols represented power, force, and of course the male. These could be everything from towers, obelisks, snakes and serpents, the stems of flowers, knives and blades, and tall mountain peaks. The female aspect was all about concave images that were receptive, such as cups, vases, ponds, hollow places, lakes, and the womb. Freud also associated certain activities such as dancing and riding a horse with sexual pleasure, especially when women were engaging in such acts!

There are images and concepts understood all over the world to mean more than what they do on the surface. Both the subconscious mind and the collective unconscious recognize these powerful motifs and symbols on a deeper level and experience the connectedness of all of humanity through shared experiences, dreams, ideas, and visions.

Motifs

Every culture has its own origin story of the creation of the world and how we humans came to be in it. Every culture also has stories and myths about the end of the world, the great deluge/flood, the dawn of humanity, and even the fall of empires. These motifs are embedded deep within the collective unconscious of humanity as a whole, but each culture may have their own spin on the details and specifics.

Some of the more prevalent motifs include:

- Creation/origin of the world and humanity
- The great deluge/flood
- The Green Man

- The apocalypse/end of the world
- The battle between good and evil
- The Sun God
- The waters of creation/primordial soup
- The hero's journey
- Fate, destiny, and free will
- Romance and tragedy
- Retribution and revenge
- The cycle of life

These motifs are expressions of our collective understanding of how the world was created, how human beings came to be, and our individual place in the larger and grander scheme of things. Though names, dates, and locations may change, the ultimate foundation of these motifs stays the same the entire world over.

One example is the great flood/deluge, which appears in the Old Testament of the Bible as the story of Noah and his ark, but also serves as the backdrop for the far older Mesopotamian *Epic of Gilgamesh*. A flood story in the Hindu *Satapatha Brahmana* features the first man, Manu, being warned about a coming flood. He is even told to build a boat![9] The Chinese Gun-You myth tells of a father and son who are tasked with controlling the flood, and another Chinese myth, the Hei Miao, is the story of a flood brought about when angry thunder decided to drown the Earth and only two humans survived to continue the species![10]

This global recurring motif tells us that a great flood must have occurred around a particular time period, although each culture has its own way of documenting the event and the experiences with varying deities, characters, and locations. The regional may differ, but the global is the same.

Dreams

Both Freud and Jung were proponents of dream symbolism and interpretation as an important aspect of psychoanalysis, though they differed in how to interpret dreams. Obviously, Jung moved toward looking for universal and archetypal imagery and symbols more than Freud did, and the appearance of his many archetypes in a dream meant something powerful to the subconscious and collective unconscious parts of the mind. The conscious mind does not speak the language of dreams, for it is analytical and reason-oriented. But, in dreams, the "other minds" get the chance to communicate and they do so with imagery.

Freud, who wrote his seminal *The Interpretation of Dreams* in 1900, chose to look at dreams from the *object level* as a relationship between the dreamer and the people and situations in the dream. Jung focused on the *subject level*, the symbolic revelations of the dream of the individual's psychological life and inner transformations. An example would be dreaming of one's mother, which would, in Jungian dream analysis, be about the anima of the dreamer, the feminine side. It can also suggest a connection to a "motherland" or a "mothering" aspect of behavior. This way of looking at symbolism in dreams as archetypal is what most divided Jung from Freud in their respective theories. Freud also identified "wish fulfillment" as a motivation for dreams, whereas Jung felt that a limiting explanation. To Jung, dream symbols were to be interpreted against a larger, more expansive view of consciousness itself, and he even suggested that it would be impossible to come up with a definitive meaning for a dream without first understanding the dreamer and his/her situation.[11]

There is so much debate surrounding the meaning behind dreams, and that is because there is a lot of subjectivity and individualism involved. What this author of this book dreams about may be different from what the readers do, and yet there will be those common motifs, themes, and elements. By becoming more aware of what we dream, even writing down dreams upon awakening (more on that later), we can begin to get a glimpse of the hidden landscape within that drives and programs much of our thoughts, actions, and behaviors.

Analysis of dreams has no doubt occurred since the dawn of humanity, when our primitive ancestors tried to understand the complex scenarios, often nonsensical, playing out in their night-time minds. Although some dreams are pretty easy to ascribe to an actual fear, person, event, or situation (for example, a hunter dreaming of being eaten by a bear the same night he is attacked by one), there is often the need to dig a little deeper. Sometimes, a double meaning is implied, such as dreaming of a person you love, but in the dream the person is evil. This could represent not only his/her darker aspects you are denying, but also your own hatred for that side of him/her.

There are other theories about how to interpret dreams, ascribing them to human instinct, biological functions, and even sexuality.

When it comes to archetypes working in our lives, though, certainly we can recognize many already listed, but one of the most obvious examples comes in the form of motifs in recurring dreams. Recurring dreams haunt us and offer rich opportunity, if examined and interpreted properly, for understanding what we are afraid of, challenged by, and love. Dreams may be blunt in their obviousness, or use metaphor to convey a message to the dreamer. Recurring dreams emphasize an importance that, if paid attention to, can lead to transformational effects and even healing!

Some recurring dream motifs are:

- Plane crashes: can signify a sense of loss of control over one's life, or that one is on a "crash and burn" course and there is a need for a change in the flight pattern/ direction.
- Tidal waves, tornados, and natural disasters: can be related of course to a disaster just experienced, but often

represent a loss of control over one's surroundings and environment, and a pending sense of "disaster" in a relationship, job, or even health.

- Being chased or attacked: most dreams involving being chased can signify a sense of the past trying to catch up with the dreamer. Perhaps big mistakes or bad decisions are plaguing the conscious mind and appear as an attacker trying to catch the dreamer in the dream. Often these involve hiding, but knowing the attacker can see you, as if there is no escaping the past.

- Being pregnant/having a baby: for men and women, these dreams may be about new beginnings. Children are archetypes of potentiality and possibility.

- Being naked: do you fear being exposed or being seen for who you really are? Nudity in a dream is not about wanting to be an exhibitionist, but about dealing with feelings of being vulnerable and exposed, even judged and shamed.

- Teeth: there is some consensus among dream symbol guides that dreaming of losing teeth is a fear of growing older.

- Being trapped: obviously about a feeling of being trapped by certain aspects of life, such as a bad marriage, a lousy job, or bad health.

- Dying: though few people actually die in dreams, the act of dying is popular and is said to signify fear of great changes. Of course, it can also represent the archetypal fear all humanity shares of mortality, but the way one dies in a dream is important to note and could help identify areas of change needed.

- Being back in school/taking a test: symbolizes our deep-rooted fear of not performing well, doing well in public, or completing a task. It can also mean feeling insecure and unprepared for life or an upcoming situation such as a job interview.

- Talking animals: symbolize guides offering wisdom, direction, or support.

- Flying: one of the most popular recurring situational archetypes, and is said to represent everything from a desire for freedom, a sense of not being grounded, and the expression of sexuality. Or maybe we humans just want to fly!

Any dream that we have again and again offers valuable insight into our own psyches. The images that stay with us are important, otherwise our brain would dream them, cycle through them, and move on. Jung also believed, as he wrote in "The Structure of the Psyche" in 1917, that an understanding of myth and mythology could help lend to an understanding of dreams. Both are ripe with archetypal images, people, and situations. Both come from the well of the collective unconscious, which is why dreams are said to be myths of the sleeping mind.[12]

In *Man and His Symbols*, Carl Jung writes in "Approaching the Unconscious" that "dream symbols are for the most part manifestations of a psyche that is beyond the control of the conscious mind. Meaning and purposefulness are not prerogatives of the mind: they operate in the whole of living nature..." He compared this to the growth of a plant, which produces a flower. The growth of the psyche, by a similar process, creates its symbols.[13]

As our species evolves, we may be creating the archetypes of the present, to be studied and interpreted in the future. Those who take on the task will wonder what our symbols meant and why they were so important to us. Imagine a cell phone as the future archetype of global connectivity, as researchers pore over our texts, emojis, and computer lingo to find out who we were so they can understand the collective unconscious of our times!

In an upcoming chapter we will examine ways to work with dreams, especially in a lucid state, and how it can help us learn more about who we are and what we need to pay attention to so that we don't repeat negative patterns.

[chapter 4]

Global Archetypes: Pop Culture, Politics, and the Collective World View

Why do we love certain movies, television shows, and fictional stories? Why do some characters leap off the page and others fall flat? How do writers, artists, and creators come up with images that sear into our collective memories? They all use, knowingly or not, archetypes in their work. By appealing to the deepest parts of our psyches and those symbols that are universal to all, creators can not only reach bigger audiences, but also influence and affect them.

Archetypes in pop culture mirror those within the individual and collective. Art usually imitates life and vice versa. But it goes beyond the things that entertain us, as we find these archetypes in business, politics, and religion, for better or worse. No matter the world stage, symbols create the stage itself and the players who move and act upon it all do so within the unconscious confines of the stage.

Politics and Leadership

A quick look at the political landscape of the world reveals heroes, villains, martyrs, saints, devils, and a host of other archetypes. Dictators get to play the role of villain and devil, with revolutionaries taking on the more heroic and sometimes "messiah" roles. Presidents and premiers might be looked upon as heroic if they do more good than harm. Or they might become the outcasts if caught in scandal and corruption. It's pretty easy to fill in the blanks when it comes to specific figures throughout human history that have played these rather symbolic roles.

We tend to separate the good from the bad, leaving the neutral aside because they aren't as flashy to the collective psyche. Jesus, Mohammed, Buddha, Moses, Krishna, and a host of religious leaders and figures from history fall into the hero/wise one/messiah categories, as well as the "chosen one" archetype (although there will be pockets of those who see them as the "enemy" from their perspective). Political figures such as Hitler, Mussolini, Pol Pot, and others are to us the "devil in the flesh" and represent every dark aspect of humanity expressed. John F. Kennedy, Robert F. Kennedy, Martin Luther King Jr., Princess Diana, and other world figures take on a more "golden" role of heroism, goodness, and honor (although, again, there will be those who see the opposite).

Every election cycle, no matter the country, the populace must choose between different archetypal figures (or, sadly, the same in different clothing!) to run said country. Unfortunately, most of us are trained only to use our conscious minds to respond to the speeches, platforms, and positions of politicians, without ever paying attention to those nudgings of the gut that point to something deeper we should be paying attention to.

The power of the personal subconscious, unconscious and, on a grander scale, the collective unconscious, could possibly change the outcome of world events and the global direction, but only when the masses become aware of the symbols operating beneath the exterior gloss and shine. An example of this is referenced in *Man and His Symbols*, in a section written by M.L. von Franz, about the "dark side." Because we look to world leaders to, well, lead us, it is critical we look at both their public persona and for evidence of the darker shadow of their "self" that may be operating their beliefs and actions. Von Franz writes, "The dark side of the Self is the most dangerous thing of all, precisely because the Self is the greatest power in the psyche. It can cause people to 'spin' megalomanic or other delusory fantasies that catch them up and 'possess' them."

He goes on to say that someone in this process will believe he/she has "grasped and solved the great cosmic riddle" and loses all sense of reality. Looking at many world leaders, whether in religion or politics, through the course of human history, many come to mind who went down this very path often to the detriment and death of millions.[1]

Why is this important? Because in order to transform society, just as with self-transformation, we must look to that collective unconscious to see why things are the way they are. The goal of course is to change the world, but it is impossible to do so without examining the symbols the world operates by.

In *The Vision Thing: Myth, Politics and Psyche in the World*, Thomas Singer writes about the power of vision and how the lack of it can create chaos and disassociation between the public and the leaders it chooses. But to work, that vision must be linked to myth, which in turn is linked to the collective unconscious. "There are times when politicians stumble into the need to link the political to the mythological. They are propelled by a peculiar mix of dire necessity, conscious intention, and a deep unconscious sense of collective mind," he writes. Singer looks at President George Bush and the "winning" of the Gulf War, who then thought he was unbeatable. He lost to Bill Clinton and much of the reason why could be his lack of communicating with the electorate in a way that mattered: "The President had lost touch with everyday life and people in his own country. His re-election campaign began to implode. Bush identified part of his problem connecting with a restless electorate as 'the vision thing.'"

Though Bush recognized the problem, it was too late to tap into that collective vision as many world leaders have done. Martin Luther King's "I have a dream" speech became itself an archetype of freedom. John F. Kennedy's "Ask not what your country can do for you, but what you can do for your country" phrase also resonated on that deep, unconscious level with a populace desperate for meaning and purpose. Singer states, "Vision is seen with the mind's or spirit's eye…it is the rare leader who can articulate a true vision that fits with real politics."[2]

As we are about to see with pop culture, and our own "stories" of our lives, the world stage appears to follow its own journey, ripe with archetypal symbols, of birth-death-rebirth, of initiation into a hero's journey complete with obstacles, challenges, and guides along the way. What we go through alone is mirrored in the collective, and when we transform the individual, we can transform the collective. Archetypes can be changed for both, as we will see.

First, however, why did you go see *Star Wars* again and again? Why do you love television shows like *The Walking Dead* and *Game of Thrones* to the point of weeping over the deaths of characters and, in some extreme cases, breaking television sets! Why do we love certain characters, certain plotlines, themes, and narratives more than others? Why do some pop culture phenomena transcend gender, race, culture, and even time, becoming a part of the fabric of human experience?

The answer, my friend, is blowing in the wind. Not really. It's because the most popular, universal, memorable, endearing, enlightening, empowering, gut-punching, and life-changing forms of entertainment contain archetypes that speak to us in the soul, as well as the mind and heart.

Popular Culture

In pop culture, the hero is the most popular archetype, and that makes sense. We all want to be the heroes of our own lives, especially when the hero in the book or show comes from a less than positive background, fights adversity, and wins the day. We can relate on a massive scale. Not many would relate to the hero symbol if he or she was just plain perfect and lucky. Those characteristics are not universal enough. Even the anti-hero is somewhat relatable, but not on the massive scale of the hero. We are drawn to what we aspire to be.

Other popular symbols are the villain, the trickster, the guide/ mentor, and the sidekick, but as we can see from the following list, archetypes of all kinds abound. This is not an exhaustive list by any means, but it becomes quite obvious that the entertainment that goes down in history as being either influential, popular, or both contains the power of archetypes at its core. Some of these are listed by the actor/actress names and some by character, whichever is more recognizable.

Hero
- Bilbo and Frodo Baggins of *The Lord of the Rings* and *Hobbit* franchises
- Luke Skywalker, Han Solo, Princess Leia, and Rey of the *Star Wars* film series
- Spiderman, Superman, Wonder Woman, et al.
- Indiana Jones
- Harry Potter
- Katniss Everdeen from *The Hunger Games* franchise

Anti-hero

- Roland Deschain of *The Dark Tower* series by Stephen King
- Bruce Wayne in *The Dark Knight*
- Rick Grimes in *The Walking Dead*
- Ishmael and Captain Ahab in *Moby Dick*
- Matt Murdock of *Daredevil*, and possibly Frank Castle (*The Punisher*)

Villain

- Darth Vader, the Emperor, et al. from the *Star Wars* films
- The Governor, Gareth, and Negan in *The Walking Dead*
- Randall Flagg from Stephen King's *The Dark Tower* and *Stand* novels
- Dr. Evil from the *Austin Powers* franchise
- The wolf in "Three Little Pigs"

Lover

- Johnny Depp as *Don Juan DeMarco*
- Warren Beatty in *Shampoo*
- Guinevere and Sir Lancelot of the King Arthur romances
- Kristin Scott Thomas and Ralph Fiennes in *The English Patient*
- Bella and Edward in the *Twilight* book series

Femme Fatale

- Catwoman
- Kathleen Turner in *Body Heat*
- Elizabeth Taylor as *Cleopatra*
- Scarlett O'Hara in *Gone With the Wind*

- Sharon Stone in *Basic Instinct*
- Glenn Close in *Fatal Attraction*

Trickster

- Bugs Bunny
- Lucy of *I Love Lucy*
- The Road Runner
- Tyrion Lannister in *Game of Thrones*
- Joey and Chandler on *Friends*

Mentor

- Yoda and Obi-Wan Kenobi of the *Star Wars* films
- Alice of *The Brady Bunch*
- Hershel in *The Walking Dead*
- Fagin in *Oliver Twist*
- Sidney Poitier in *To Sir, With Love*

The Explorer

- Jodie Foster in *Contact*
- Dana Scully and Fox Mulder in *The X-Files*
- Indiana Jones
- Nancy Drew and the Hardy Boys
- Alice in *The Adventures of Alice in Wonderland*
- Dorothy in *The Wizard of Oz*

Boy/Girl Next Door

- The cast of *Friends*
- Gidget
- Marshall in *How I Met Your Mother*

- Molly Ringwald in *Pretty in Pink*
- Janet on *Three's Company*

Rebel

- James Dean
- Marlon Brando in *The Wild One*
- Sally Field in *Norma Rae*
- Julia Roberts in *Erin Brockovich*
- Han Solo in the *Star Wars* films
- Daryl in *The Walking Dead*

Sidekicks

- Fred and Ethel Mertz from *I Love Lucy*
- R2-D2, C-3PO, and other droids from the *Star Wars* films
- Snoopy in the *Charlie Brown* franchise
- Chrissie and Larry on *Three's Company*
- The Cowardly Lion, Tin Man, and Scarecrow of *The Wizard of Oz*
- Iago in *Othello* by Shakespeare

Visionary

- Greer Garson as *Madame Curie*
- Noah Wylie/Michael Fassbinder as *Steve Jobs*
- Merlin in the King Arthur romances
- Herschel and Dale in *The Walking Dead*
- Yoda and Obi-Wan in the *Star Wars* films

Warrior

- John Wayne in *The Searchers*
- Mel Gibson's *Braveheart*

- King Arthur
- Roland Deschain of *The Dark Tower* series
- Rick, Michonne, Carol, Maggie, Glenn, Daryl, Carl, Morgan, et al. in *The Walking Dead*

Though this list could feature hundreds of characters and pop culture references, it gives us a solid idea of how important and prevalent archetypes are and how they speak to the universal experiences we also hope to experience when we open a novel or attend a movie. Some characters display more than one archetype, or evolve from one into another during the course of their time on the screen or the pages of a book. Ideally, the most universal characters should grow and change, hopefully for the better. In the case of some heroes, they may also display characteristics of villains. Rick Grimes of *The Walking Dead* is a perfect example of a hero archetype who is also a villain and anti-hero because of the tactics he chooses to protect his family and fellow survivors. For those who have not watched the show, he is a brilliant examination of a man torn between what is right and moral and what needs to be done, and often the two do not meet in the middle.

It's a fun exercise to look at pop culture and find the archetypes. Those shows that resonated the most with audiences are always the most obvious, even if the subject matter of the show was pure silliness. Take *Gilligan's Island*, for example, created by Sherwood Schwartz in 1964. The show's theme song has become iconic, but it was the characters that lived on long after the final season ended. To this day, the show is in reruns and the archetypes of the seven leads are quite obviously part of the enduring charm.

Gilligan: the innocent child, the trickster, and the fool.

The Skipper: the father and the mentor.

The Professor: the visionary, the mentor, and the genius.

Mr. Howell: the king.

Mrs. Howell: the queen.

Ginger Grant: the femme fatale.

Mary Ann Summers: the girl next door.

Even the cast of the more modern *Friends*, which ran 10 seasons and was created by David Crane and Marla Kauffman, features archetypal characters we immediately connect and resonate with, even if we ourselves are not like them. We certainly know people who are!

Monica Geller: girl next door, mother, and queen.

Ross Geller: king, lover, father, and visionary.

Chandler Bing: boy next door, sidekick, and fool.

Joey Tribbiani: child, jester, trickster, lover, and sidekick.

Phoebe Buffay: rebel, artist, and sidekick.

Rachel Green: princess, girl next door, and lover.

Do you love the King Arthur stories of chivalry and heroism? That's because they are filled with archetypes, both personal and situational, to form a classic story that has been repeated again and again as the basis for other "heroic" films.

King Arthur: king, hero, leader, visionary, and messiah.

Merlin: mentor, magician, sage, and wizard.

Queen Guinevere: queen, lover, betrayer, and warrior.

Morgana Le Fey: witch, queen, temptress, and femme fatale.

Sir Lancelot: hero, lover, betrayer, and warrior.

Sir Perceval: hero, innocent, child, warrior, and explorer.

Mordred: shadow, betrayer, and villain.

A more modern version of the King Arthur tale is mirrored in the *Star Wars* film franchise, with kings and queens, heroes and heroines, and mentors and sidekicks galore. Fashioned on the archetypes that most affect people and hold universal appeal, it's easy for audiences to love and hate characters that resonate on a collective and unconscious level. The first movie, released in 1977, was *A New Hope* and along with several later installments introduced perhaps the most archetypal figures in motion picture history, a few of which are listed below!

Han Solo: king, hero, leader, trickster, and explorer.

Princess Leia Organa: hero, leader, queen, warrior, and mother.

Luke Skywalker: hero, innocent, child, explorer, and initiate.

Obi-Wan Kenobi: mentor, guide, sage, and teacher.

Yoda: mentor, guide, sage, and teacher.

Darth Vader: villain, leader, shadow, and king (dark).

C-3PO and R2-D2: sidekicks, jesters, heroes, and tricksters.

At the writing of this book, the most popular and widely viewed television show is Robert Kirkman's *The Walking Dead*, a story of humans trying to survive a zombie apocalypse and their fellow humans, the latter often presenting more of a danger than the zombies. The massive success of a "zombie" series is the appeal of the characters, many whom successfully blend archetypes, especially the hero/anti-hero, because of the need for the heroes to often resort to the same brutality as their proclaimed enemies. Just a few of the key archetypal characters are:

Rick Grimes: hero, anti-hero, leader, warrior, and father.

Carl Grimes: hero, child, innocent, initiate, and warrior.

Daryl Dixon: hero, anti-hero, rebel, warrior, and lone wolf.

Michonne: hero, queen, mother, warrior, leader, and diplomat.

Herschel: visionary, leader, mentor, guide, and sage.

Carol: survivor, victim, warrior, mother, and lone wolf.

Morgan: sage, warrior, magician, diplomat, and peacemaker.

Glenn Rhee: hero, innocent, warrior, lover, and prince.

Maggie Rhee: hero, innocent, lover, princess, and leader.

The Governor: villain, anti-hero, father, leader, and false messiah.

Negan: villain, leader, dictator, false messiah, and devil.

Once we become aware of the archetypes in pop culture, it's hard to not immediately recognize them. The success of a novel, short story, movie, television show, or any other form of creative expression can often be pinpointed back to the use of archetypes that we most identify with, including the aspects of ourselves we deny and suppress, such as the shadow, villain, and betrayer. Pop culture allows us to see those aspects and vicariously express and process them in a way that we aren't even aware of because they are working on the collective unconscious level.

There are also situation archetypes in pop culture; for example, the plots of many movies and novels are themselves symbolic and universal. The most popular of these is the hero's journey. Joseph Campbell wrote *The Hero with a Thousand Faces* in 1949, documenting his theory of the archetypal journey of the hero figure that is found in world myths, fairy tales, and now, popular fictional storytelling. This is known as a "monomyth," for it is a unifying concept found throughout cultures and belief systems on a global scale.[3] The best-known modern example of the hero's journey in action is the *Star Wars* franchise because George Lucas, the creator, was an avid follower of Campbell's works. The hero's journey is also prevalent in movies such as *The Wizard of Oz*, the *Hobbit* franchise, *The Lion King*, and *Close Encounters of the Third Kind*, as well as television series, novels, comics, and other forms of storytelling.

The Hero's Journey

Even aside from pop culture, myth, and fairy tale, many of us can identify the stages of our own hero's journey, which consists of between 12 and 17 steps, depending on where you look. The following template comes from the work of Christopher Vogler, author of the 1985 book, *A Practical Guide to Joseph Campbell's "The Hero with a Thousand Faces,"* who has taught the hero's journey archetype to filmmakers and writers alike in his college course as "The Writer's Journey." We are using this template in particular because in a later chapter we will be writing our own stories. The hero's journey is the foundation upon which great stories are built, and though the pattern may vary, the basics stay the same.[4]

1. The Ordinary World

    The ordinary world is the beginning, where the hero (male or female) lives. It is often plain, dull, and uneventful, and the hero feels the urge toward wanderlust.

2. The Call to Adventure

    Something calls the hero away from their ordinary world and onto the path of adventure. The hero is usually reluctant to leave the comforts of home, but they must, for it is their destiny to do so. They enter a new world, different, intimidating, and even filled with dangers and obstacles.

3. Refusal of the Call/Quest

    The hero is tasked with a challenge that only he/she can complete. The hero can either accept it or deny their destiny. When the hero accepts, the stage is set and they make the commitment to move forward.

4. Meeting the Mentor

    The hero meets a guide or mentor who trains, advises, and equips him/her for the rest of the journey.

5. Entering the Unknown/Crossing the Threshold

    The hero enters the strange new world where the path to their destiny leads them. It may be filled with supernatural beings, possible danger, and even death, but the hero moves forward and begins to learn the lay of the land.

6. Allies, Enemies, and Challenges/Tests

    At this point, the hero finds allies along the path, but also enemies and tests that he/she must complete to move forward. Often, allies come in the form of supernatural aid or even special talismans.

7. The Approach to the Innermost Cave

    The hero comes to a cave or underground place filled with danger. This is where the hero must go to face and overcome his/her innermost fears, including death.

8. The Supreme Ordeal

   The hero hits bottom, the abyss, facing death and perhaps a mythical beast or demon. The hero symbolically dies and is born again, newly empowered.

9. The Reward/Seizing the Sword

   The hero is given a treasure after facing death that he/she must deliver home or somewhere special.

10. The Journey Back Home

    The hero begins the long journey back home with the treasure in hand, and may be chased by the enemy at this point. The mission of the hero becomes more urgent.

11. Resurrection

    The hero is almost home, when the biggest test of all is given. A final sacrifice purifies the hero; there is death and rebirth on a higher, deeper level, and the hero's actions heal the polarities and balance the scales. Conflict is resolved. The hero is born anew, this time for good.

12. Return Home

    The hero goes home with the treasure or some special element that can transform the world. The hero has also been transformed.

Joseph Campbell's actual hero's journey template was more complex than Vogler's. Divided into three parts—the departure, the initiation, and the return—it contains 17 steps that can be found in some variation in the world's myths, religious stories, fairy tales, folk tales, as well as in modern pop culture:

1. Departure
2. The Call to Adventure

3. Refusing the Call

4. Supernatural Aid

5. Crossing the Threshold

6. The Belly of the Whale

7. Initiation

8. The Road of Trials

9. The Meeting with Goddess

10. Tempted by Woman

11. Atonement with the Father

12. Apotheosis

13. The Ultimate Boon

14. Return

15. Refusal of Return

16. The Magic Flight

17. Rescue From Without

18. The Crossing of the Return Threshold

19. Master of Two Worlds

20. Freedom to Live[5]

Campbell's 1949 monomyth sits at the heart of many of the greatest stories, not just about specific heroes, but society as well. In *The American Monomyth: Myth of the American Superhero* written in 1977 by John Shelton Lawrence and Robert Jewett, the authors suggest a common template to many of the most endearing "hero" stories we recognize throughout history: "A community in a harmonious paradise is threatened by evil; normal institutions fail to contend with this threat; a selfless superhero emerges to renounce temptations and carry out the redemptive task; aided by fate, his decisive victory restores the community to its paradisiacal condition; the superhero then recedes into obscurity."[6]

Sound familiar?

Like the foundation of a house, different stories can lead to different windows and doors, but the structure itself is the same. Some creative artists choose to work with archetypal characters or situations on purpose, knowing how much they will add to the appeal of their work. Others find that the inclusion is something organic and that it naturally evolves out of the story itself.

The author of this book interviewed writers to find out just how important archetypes are to their own work. What follows are insights into the minds of creators and how they view their characters and work to create memorable stories with universal elements.

Looking into the processes used by writers and artists helps us become aware of archetypes we resonate with, relate to, and are repelled by, and why. There is incredible insight into why some of us hate victim characters and others feel compassion for them. The way we respond to characters and themes in pop culture is a mirror for what is going on in our own lives.

Whether in a book, on a big or small screen, or in a fairy tale of old, characters and situations that speak to us on a universal level have the potential to affect our lives the most. In the grid of interconnectivity that is the collective unconscious, information and symbols, images and stories, themes and messages all have the ability to spread like wildfire, or "go viral," and influence millions, even billions of people. Yet they do it so subtly, beneath the radar of the critical and analytical mind, that their impact is more profound.

But someone else's story is someone else's story. What about the stories we create about our own lives? And, if we are living a story that we don't like or no longer serves our highest good or the good of humanity, can we then change it? It could be as simple as turning the page to see what happens next.

[chapter 5]

Who Are You and
What's Your Story?

"Who are you?"

Ugh. If you are anything like this author, you hate that dreaded question. Upon meeting someone new, or being introduced to those you don't know, the question always comes up. Yet few of us seem in touch enough with ourselves to be able to answer it without an awful lot of hesitation.

Why don't we know who we are?

It's easy to answer such a question with frivolous information that gives another person an idea more of how we spend our time than who we truly are.

"I'm a writer and mom and owner of a Chihuahua."

"I'm an accountant and hockey fan who loves his wife and kids."

"I'm an artist who works full-time as a waiter to support my true calling."

"I'm a breast cancer survivor and I own my own tax preparation business."

We give little hints of who we are at our core, but somehow think that by sharing the deeper aspects of our identity we might scare others away. Imagine diving a little deeper next time the question pops up.

"I'm a creative dreamer who wants to use the power of my words and stories to change lives and make myself feel purposeful."

"I'm a survivor and a thriver who can take on any challenge and overcome it, thanks to my battle with cancer."

"I'm a drug addict trying to get clean, but alienated from my family for not being able to do so yet."

"I'm a former exotic dancer now doing what I truly love, teaching autistic children music and dance to get them to express themselves."

These explanations are more about labeling ourselves, based upon the stories of our lives, and for which we use symbols to convey. We don't want to bore anyone with a 10-hour lecture about who we believe we are and how we got to those beliefs, so we punctuate our own "hero's journey" with labels, even symbols, that we figure others will relate to. These include:

Survivor

Mother

Businessperson

Creative artist

Athlete

College student

Abuse victim

Doctor

Animal lover

The list is inexhaustible.

Your Archetypes

Make a list of every archetype you believe yourself to be. Include the good with the bad because they all work to make the image of "you" that you not only buy into, but present to the world. Write them down and add a few reasons why you identify with each aspect of your personality. You may end up with a list like this:

Warrior: I've fought a bad marriage, cancer, and job loss and I'm still standing.

Leader: I always step up to lead my community groups and school PTO, and worked in HR.

King: I am a great father and provider to my family.

Jester: I always use humor and levity in challenging situations.

Fool: I was a fool for love a few times in my past.

Father: I raise my children with love and guidance.

Rebel: I left a crappy corporate job to become a novelist.

Make the list as extensive and honest as you can because before you can change anything about yourself, you have to admit to who your *self* is—at least your interpretation of *self*. It may be helpful to ask close friends and family how they see you, too, because you might be blind to both good and bad aspects that have become habitual and ingrained.

Don't scrimp on the negative aspects. These archetypes are the exact symbols that you most want to examine and possibly alter or eradicate. There can be no dishonesty and avoidance when working on self-improvement. Are you a *worrywart*? Are you a *saboteur* of your own success and happiness? Have you acted as a *betrayer* to yourself or others? Are you a *cheater* or a *thief*? Do you *destroy* more than you *create?* Have others called you Lazy Jane, Negative Ned, or Downer Debbie?

Once you feel your list is complete, take a look at the archetypes and cross out those that are positive, beneficial, and empowering to you. Those that remain will be the aspects of your psyche and personality that will be worked on later. Some of the archetypes on your list may be either/or. For example, if you listed survivor because you fought breast cancer and are now in remission, can you possibly find a way to make that a more powerful archetype at work in your life by replacing it with thriver? For many survivors of disease and other traumas, the word "survivor" often doesn't necessarily mean they are living a good and happy life; rather, just surviving and staying alive. Ask yourself if you just want to continue to survive, or thrive, prosper, and be healthy and strong.

Are you a natural guide, but want to become more of a mentor? Leave guide on the list so that you can then replace it later with a more purposeful archetype that reflects a dream or new desire to help others. The idea with this list is to get real and true on what aspects you want to keep and allow to evolve, and what aspects have run their course and overstayed their welcome. It does no one any good to hold onto old archetypes out of guilt, need, or worry that if we let go of them, we will be lost and without purpose. There comes a time in every life when the "initiate" becomes the "leader" or the "princess" graduates into a "queen."

Look at every archetype and see if there is a better and more powerful symbol you could replace it with. Even if you don't quite yet know what that replacement is, just leave the archetype on the list to work on later. Only you know for sure what is working in your life and what isn't. If there is any hesitation, leave it on the list.

Before we get to the exercises in the next chapter, though, we have an even bigger job to do.

What's *Your* Story, Anyway?

So what is your story, pal? That is a question that is almost as hard to answer as "Who are you?" In fact, the answers may be the same for both questions! Because our stories begin to form in early childhood, when our awareness of self kicks in, we build page after page into the book of life, rarely looking back to see how each page got to the point of the story we are now in. Eventually, when we die, we close the book and whatever is inside is what we will be remembered as.

But what if there are parts of our stories that are not serving us in the present? What if there are pages and entire chapters that we suppressed and denied? We are now paying a price for it, even if we cannot consciously pinpoint why.

What if we don't like the story much at all because it is not our story, but the one that was imposed upon us by parents, peers, and society? Are we living out a narrative we barely have control over, or think belongs to us when it was inscribed upon our pages by so many other hands? How tragic would it be to get to the end of our lives and realize we never lived as we had wanted to? Those kinds of regrets can haunt us beyond the grave!

Imagine starting a new novel, so excited to dive into it and getting lost in the story and characters. The problem is that about 30 pages in, it just sucks. The plot is meandering and the characters are mind-numbingly boring. Any normal person would simply close the book and find another to start.

Believe it or not, we can do this with many aspects of our lives. We can look at the plot, characters, and the trajectory of the story and decide to change what isn't making us happy, healthy, and fulfilled right now. It starts with first honestly assessing our stories.

This is a time for total truth-telling because lying about our own pasts, or brushing things under the rug that we don't want to face up to, does us no good and could be doing us a whole lot of "no good." By being brutally honest about our stories, as much as we can remember them, we will begin to uncover signs, symbols, and patterns that serve us and signs, symbols, and patterns that don't.

Some people cannot remember everything that ever happened to them from the day they were born to the present, but defining moments and events are enough to show the "plotline" and give us an idea of what was driving our thoughts, actions, and behaviors. Sometimes comments people have made to us, about us, and comments we have made to ourselves can be telling: "Why do I always do everything?" "Suffer the fool in love!" "Lucky in business, not in romance." "Always giving, rarely receiving." "Tired of always carrying the family weight." "Sick and tired of being a victim." "Since I was little, he/she/they were against my dreams." "I will always be overweight and undesirable, just like in my teens."

Those little snippets of internal and external conversations are priceless for understanding why we do what we do, and behave as we behave, even when we don't like what we are doing. Once we identify the beliefs we have accumulated about who we are, we can then figure out if we were the ones who put them into play in our lives. Or was it our parents, peers, or society itself, our teachers, religious and political leaders, our lovers, friends, and colleagues, and even total strangers? Yes, even a comment made in passing from a stranger can dig deep into the psyche and cause damage to the roots, which then affects the whole plant.

We *must* identify what parts of ourselves belong to us and what was written into the books of our lives by other hands with other agendas, motives, needs, and desires. If we continue to believe and buy into the "we" that was created for us with little input of our own, then there is no way our lives can ever become more authentic. We will continue to live by the archetypes chosen by others and not those we truly feel reflect who are and envision ourselves to be. Think of it as cleaning house and getting rid of stuff that we don't want, need, or even like, especially gifts we were given by well-meaning friends and family that are not useful and might even be harmful. Although those gifts may have been given to us from people who "meant well," they still don't come from a place of deep personal authenticity. Give them away. Maybe someone else can use them!

Before we look at ways to deconstruct and then reconstruct our stories, and in the process dig up the archetypes at the roots of our behaviors, we need to find the quiet time to reflect on our story. This may be through ongoing meditation, journaling, writing, poetry, song, or any other method by which we can really go into solitude, get silent, and go back in time, making note of the people and events we feel profoundly affected us.

Perhaps talking into a recorder and retelling our story works better. Some people are writers, others are speakers. Others may want to draw it out. No matter how we do it, we must be honest, raw, and real. Change cannot come from just scratching the surface. We must dig deeper and get into the subconscious and the collective unconscious and shine light into dark corners to see what is there, lurking in the shadows, invisible yet incredibly powerful. This process may take time because we often forget so much of what happened to us in the past until we are forced to revisit it. But the more we can remember and own up to, the more effective the entire process will be in the end. When it comes to self-empowerment, there is no skimping because in many ways, the quality of our lives depends upon honest assessments.

Those familiar with Alcoholics Anonymous and other recovery programs that use the 12 steps know that one of the steps, Step Four, requires writing out a "fearless moral inventory" of all of the things the alcoholic or addict has done that apply to their disease and desire for recovery. In *The Big Book of Alcoholics Anonymous*, Step Four reads:

A business which takes no regular inventory usually goes broke. Taking commercial inventory is a fact-finding and a fact-facing process. It is an effort to discover the truth about the stock-in-trade. One object is to disclose damaged or unsalable goods, to get rid of them promptly and without regret. If the owner of the business is to be successful, he cannot fool himself about values.

We did exactly the same thing with our lives. We took stock honestly. First, we searched out the flaws in our make-up which caused our failure. Being convinced that self, manifested in various ways, was what had defeated us, we considered its common manifestations.[1]

Having been through the 12-Step Program a few times, this author can attest that often having to rip oneself open and tell the brutal truth is enough to send most people running for the hills, but also running from the one thing that might finally help in the recovery process. Examining our story under a microscope, including sins, mistakes, faults, and insanities, is critical for getting to the roots of addictions. The same level of honesty can work wonders when dealing with the past, even if we are not in some kind of recovery. It is all about looking for the beginnings of patterns of behavior we took on and are still causing us pain and suffering, and symbols we adopted or empowered that are now no longer working for us as they did in the past.

Why is this honest digging necessary? Because if we feel we have been victims all our lives, that victim archetype is on overdrive in our unconscious, pushing us into actions and behaviors that are hurting us and everyone around us. Often, the patterns created around the presence of that archetype lead us to believe once a victim, always a victim, even if this belief operates on a subconscious level and, thus, attracts more situations into our lives that *allow us to continue the pattern of being the victim!* Once we have overcome those patterns, we will stop being victims and stop hearing those around us claim, "Stop being the victim!" or "You're always playing the victim."

Ever heard the phrase, "You can never get enough of what you don't want"? This is the life we get if we don't dig up those archetypes, shine up the ones we like, and change or toss out the crusty, rusty, dingy ones that are continuing patterns we wish to stop. Until we do, we will continue to get more of what we don't want, bitch and complain about it, and then say we are tired of dealing with it.

"I'm sick and tired of..."

Try filling in the rest of that sentence. It's a powerful way to see what old, outdated archetypes are running in a loop inside of our minds!

We have to reread our stories. We have to look at who we have come to be, how we came to be, and what influences along the way were not ours and did not serve the deepest dreams we started off with as innocent children. Rereading and revisiting our stories is the beginning of the journey we all must take to wholeness and we will never truly find or live our purpose without going through this process. The good news is we don't have to just focus on the bad stuff such as our defects of character, our mistakes, sins, and transgressions because our stories would be incomplete without the good and even the neutral stuff. But it is the bad we wish to change in order to experience more of the good.

Because the concept of revisiting our entire life story is somewhat daunting, there are ways to make it easier. One is to follow Joseph Campbell's "Hero's Journey" template in the previous chapter. Another is the Vogler version used in "The Writer's Journey," which can be a tremendous help in identifying the key plot points of our stories.

Yet another method is to honestly look at what isn't working in life and "back-engineer" to the origin points of where each aspect of dissatisfaction, unhappiness, or sense of being lost began. In the next chapter we will get into some actual exercises to do this and more, but for now, let's read our stories over again.

In *Change Your Story, Change Your Life*, author and clinical psychologist Carl Greer works with Jungian archetypes and shamanic tools to help readers achieve personal transformation by recognizing our power as the storytellers of our own narratives. Working with Source energy, Greer shows readers how to use specific tools to work on existing archetypal energies and either change them or learn how to interpret them differently. His method includes shamanic journeying, dream-work, the use of ritual and ceremony, and journaling, but his emphasis is on being honest and truthful during the entire process and taking responsibility for our power in it.

"Sometimes we become so identified with our stories, so certain that we can't live according to a different one, that it seems as if the story is dictating itself to us. The truth is that none of us is our story, and each of us has the power to be the storyteller," writes Greer. It is so empowering to realize that we do have the ability to change not just the narrative, but the key symbols and players within that narrative that manifest in archetypal energies and symbols. Greer does point out that we have written part of our story on our own, but that Source is also a key player. So we must focus on what we can change and we must do it no matter how painful it is: "The thought of looking honestly at our stories may be too agonizing for us to bear, causing us to live in denial and resist reflection and self-examination."[2]

Even if we cannot recall much of our past, we can look at the present and see what is keeping us from being happy and fulfilled, and use that information as a guide to what is not working and needs attending to. There is no deadline for doing this deep inner work, except the one desired for personal transformation. Sometimes it is a slow process, but there is no judge watching over anyone to make sure this kind of work is done on time and perfectly. So tell the archetypal judge within to chill out!

Objectify the Past

Another problem we are sure to encounter when we look back upon our past is the battle between interpretation versus fact. The way we remember certain people, events, and circumstances from our past may *not* be the way they really were or how they actually happened. Our perception and emotion taints them. Our current situation casts shadows on the memories and even adds to them things we never actually experienced. We spin the past to suit how we felt at the time, or how we think we felt at the time, based upon how we now feel. This is not to say our personal interpretations, emotions, and reactions to events are wrong, but often it helps to draw up two columns:

1. What happened.

2. How we felt about it, interpreted it, and responded to it.

This exercise alone is a powerful way to really see how we may have backed ourselves into an "archetypal corner" of believing something about ourselves that may not have been true. These beliefs may still be driving our thoughts, actions, and behaviors today, years and years after the actual event occurred. Our minds love to recreate events as if they happened one way, when others who may have been present at the time will tell us they happened entirely differently.

For example, say your father left your family when you were five years old and never came back. He never contacted you again. This traumatizing experience was so awful, and rightly so, that it created deep beliefs that cripple you even today, 40 or 50 years later.

1. What happened.

   My father left the family and was never heard from again. My mom raised us [and this can be reversed to the mother leaving].

2. How I felt about it, interpreted it, and responded to it.

   I felt betrayed and abandoned by the very person who was supposed to love me. I felt useless and worthless and started acting out as a teenager, especially with men. I became a lifelong victim, afraid of love and being abandoned, so I just grew cold and shut down my heart, or I hurt and abandoned people first before they could do it to me. I became bitter and angry. I never went after my dreams because of fear of rejection.

The next question would be, just because your father abandoned you, does that mean you are not worthy of love? Does the action of your father mean you are useless or a victim? Those labels are ones placed upon ourselves, by ourselves. We didn't know how to better interpret then the heartbreaking actions of another human being, and one that caused so much trauma to the entire family.

What if the reason your father left is because he went off to war and died a hero? He couldn't come back because he had died, but in no way did that mean he did not love and adore his family. In fact, in his mind, he may have believed he was fighting *for* his family and their freedoms. Yet we take bits and pieces of the past and run with them, and they become who we are even if they weren't entirely true. But we took on the *abandoned child* and *victim* archetypes because of it and never looked back, when in fact we were neither. We were sadly just the *child* that lost the *father* to a war.

Perhaps we proposed to the woman of our dreams, only to have her reject us. We take on the role of rejected lover and refuse to ever get close to another woman again for fear of being hurt. But what if the woman rejected us because she was dying of cancer and had only two months left to live? She rejected us so that we could instead find someone who we would build a family with and not experience the suffering and grief of mourning her death. Or what if she rejected us because she was really a lesbian and was not ready to come out to anyone yet?

The rejection still hurts, but the different context can help us realize that we didn't need to take on such negative archetypes because of it. Taking everything into perspective about the past may not be possible because we may not have access to information involving those who have died, but we must do the best we can and certainly we can talk to other family members and friends to try to fill in some of those missing pieces of the puzzle.

Today we can look at the labels and symbols we took on, as well as the ones we projected onto the other person (villain), and see that we can create a new interpretation that serves us better as adults. "My father abandoned our family because he was a soldier going off to fight for my freedom. I am still loveable and worthy of love and every good thing. The man who left our family had to go to war and I miss him dearly, but I am whole without my father's attention and love." Even if your father was a jerk who left the family for another woman, you can still see that his actions and behaviors were indicative of the archetypes active in his life, not yours, and that you did not have to change your self-perception because of something someone else did, no matter their reasons or motives.

This is but one example of a person, event, or circumstance in our life stories we may want to "objectify" to see where we took on a symbol of something that was not true, such as the belief we are unworthy because someone else leaves us.

Another example might be a man struggling to always do the right thing and "be the hero," despite major resentment and anger toward those he is always saving. He might go back into his past to discover an adult taking on that martyr role, becoming the "hero," and adopting it as part of his archetypal make-up, even though it is killing him today. Once he realizes where he took on that symbolic character trait, he can then decide to stop saving everyone and focus more on his own self-care! He can still be the "hero," but in a smarter, more sensible way by balancing his own needs with the needs of others.

Always playing the "victim" and not sure why? Going back into the time capsule of the past can uncover the defining event when you first took on that archetype and made it your own. Perhaps you were abused, or even the victim of a violent crime. But you are still in the "victim" mode, playing out everything that particular archetype represents. What would your life be like if you could claim yourself, instead, as a "powerful survivor" or a "warrior of justice"? Can you imagine yourself as an armored knight, a Viking on horseback, or a powerful Valkyrie riding into battle? Without denying what happened to you, it is possible to reframe what you began to perceive yourself as because of what happened to you.

Objectifying the past does not mean diminishing the importance of how we felt at the time. Our responses and reactions, our emotions, and the way we processed something was the best we could do at the time with the resources and support we had available. But now is the time to heal and grow by pouring our beliefs into a filter and sifting out the dregs of attitudes and beliefs we adopted and made a part of the story of our lives, so that we can, if needed, change them.

Identify Yourself, Please!

Whenever this author hears a police officer on a television show yell out, "Identify yourself, please!" she has to laugh. Should the person respond with "I'm a single woman in my 40s who owns six cats and brews my own beer in my spare time"? Or perhaps, "I'm a Leo, and I love to jet ski and eat junk food"? Again, being asked by someone what we believe our "identity" is can be difficult. One of the best ways to look for hidden beliefs is to have someone ask you the question, "Who do you think you are?" Watch how you answer. Then ask that person how they perceive you; who they think you are based upon how well they know you. Is your answer a realistic portrayal of who you are, or is it based on the masks you put on for the public? Are you consciously aware of those masks? It helps to ask both a friend and yourself because often the answers will be quite different. But will they be the truth? Chances are, no, because we often hide behind our own masks and are so out of touch with our authenticity that we perceive them as the "real" person.

Asking who we are is almost as hard, maybe even harder, than asking what we want (a question few people can actually answer without requiring deep thought). It requires really digging deep to the core of our identity and speaking from that place. Sometimes, life has caused us to be so removed from this core that we need a little help getting back there.

Identity is a tricky thing, though, because we often don't even know all the levels of our own being. So, when asked, we identify ourselves with general statements that are usually about how we look, how old we are, what gender we are, where we came from, what we do for a living, and whether or not we have a family or spouse. Our true and authentic identities elude us if we always stay focused on the surface aspects we call our lives.

A great exercise to uncover our true identities is to write our own biographies. No, not a whole book, unless we feel called to do that, but a two- to three-page bio that lists all the things we associate with our "self" as if we were going to send it to a prospective employer. Try to be as detailed as possible, listing traits and skills, things we like and things we've accomplished, what has happened to us that framed who we are, and where we have lived, studied, and with whom.

Once we have written our bios, we can then look over them and see what stands out the most. First of all, was it hard to write about ourselves? Why? Shouldn't writing about the self be the easiest thing to write about? Yet most of us know so little about who we are and what we want, we can barely fill a page!

What are we proud of? Did we include things we are ashamed of? Why not, if they were instrumental in shaping us into who we are today? The things we didn't include in our bios are more important than what we did, because they indicate areas of our lives we deny, suppress, or just plain want to forget about. Yet those are the areas we most need to address and pay attention to.

Did we describe ourselves in ways that ring true, or in ways we want the public to see us as? Often, there is a huge gap between the two. Do we feel bad doing this exercise because we feel like we haven't done much with our lives and our bios are short and boring?

That alone is hugely telling for the rest of the work we will do in this book.

Our bios are only a few pages long, but they indicate what we think and believe is the most important information about us, especially when we write it as if we will be showing it to someone. Maybe that is not a bad idea: to show our bio to someone very close to us and ask that person if it mirrors in their eyes who we project ourselves to be?

But the truth is narrowing our life story down to a few pages drives home what we think is most important to our identities. That may be so far from the truth of who we really are, though, and thus open our eyes to just how little we know about ourselves.

Now that we have done the bios, we can also write a second bio that is all about who we think we are as others see us. This one will be shorter and often quite different from the one we write from our own perspectives. Notice any differences between the two. Once we work with our stories and our archetypes, we hope to throw out both of these bios in favor of one that truly indicates who we are—our authentic selves. That person will be the same to us as it is to others, because that's what authenticity is.

Back-Engineering

There are rumors that our government has back-engineered crashed UFOs to discover how they got here from there. Okay, those are rumors, but the idea of back-engineering something to learn about how it works and what makes it tick can work wonders when assembling the story of a life.

We start with where we are today and list the parts of us that we want to change or work on because they don't seem to be working at full capacity. Or maybe they work, but not in our favor! By going backward and looking at the things that have led us to who we don't want to be, we can become enlightened to patterns, challenges, and obstacles where we were derailed from our authentic self.

Let's take Mary. She is in her late 50s, divorced, and the mother of two children now in college. She is attractive, smart, and has a career as a manager for a large private corporation's R&D division. She owns her own home and has money in the bank. But she is lonely and cannot seem to meet anyone. She easily gets used by others, especially of the opposite sex, and finds it almost impossible to say no even to her own children, who often make demands upon her time and her money. And she hates her abusive boss, who takes credit for her work and invades her privacy at the workplace.

Mary knows she isn't fully living the life she envisions, or being the real "Mary" she knows exists down deep inside. But for the life of her, she can't seem to change her awful luck with men and with imposing boundaries.

Mary can back-engineer the times of her life when she felt used, taken advantage of, and taken for granted to the source or origin of these labels she put upon herself. So, she may write about her children going to college on her dime and not getting jobs when they easily could have. Back a little further to her divorcing a man who was narcissistic, selfish, and made her live off of an allowance until she had enough and left the marriage. Back further to her dating patterns with men before her marriage, when she said "yes" just to please the men she was seeing and was often "loved and left." Back even further all the way back to childhood and experiencing her own mother's martyrdom to Mary's belligerent, demanding, and selfish father. That is the point where Mary came to believe that being a "good woman" meant being a "martyr" and she wore that archetypal badge straight into a future of unhappiness and dissatisfaction.

Try back-engineering from the present day to the past to find that singular event or situation when you "became" something you weren't. Then go back to the "you" at that time and forgive yourself for not knowing how to better interpret or respond. You did the best you could, truly. But then be sure to tell the "old you" that you are now taking over and a new archetype is being put into place that will empower you. Say a loving and gentle goodbye to the "victim" and "martyr" and hello to the "superhero" and "warrior" within. It can make a powerful difference not just in your present, but in how you come to reinterpret the past as a series of events leading up to the new and improved you.

After we get this first huge step done (and yes, it is a lot of work), we can then go on to work with tools and techniques to dissect the parts of our stories that we never intended to tell in the first place. There is a famous Native American parable about a grandfather who is talking with his grandson, who says "I feel as though I have two wolves at war in my heart. One wolf is angry and vengeful; the other wolf is loving and compassionate. How do I know which wolf will win?" The grandfather says, "The one you feed is the one that will win."

Aha! So what we give our attention to is what grows bigger. What we continue to complain about, hate, resent, resist, deny, and suppress makes those very things grow because we are giving them our focus, whether consciously or subconsciously. It sounds easy to understand, but in order to stop feeding the wrong wolves, we need to first call them by name and then round them up out of the shadowy depths of their hiding places in the collective unconscious and decide whether or not we should cast them out of our own fairy tales.

[chapter 6]

Be This, Not That!
Tools for Transformation

We know our stories, right? We've listed the parts of who we think we are that we like and those that we want to change or get rid of. Now we need to know how to go about doing that. Working with our archetypes is done on all three levels of the mind: conscious, subconscious, and collective unconscious. Without cleaning out the basement and the first floor, we can have a top floor that appears spotless, but it's a surface clean. Or imagine building a home on top of liquid soil. No matter how lovely the home is, what it's built upon won't last and will take the whole house down one day.

The first thing we must do is take the list of archetypes we did not cross out and see how they influenced the narrative of our lives.

Plot Points

Take your list and your story and read through both a few times until signs and patterns emerge. Can you see where in your life you began to adopt some of the negative archetypes you now wish to change? Do you find the plot points in your life narrative where you were derailed from your authentic dreams because of an archetype you took on that didn't serve your higher purpose? Are there situational archetypes that you truly felt led you off in a wrong direction in the plans you had for your life?

What stands out is what needs to be worked on. A narrative filled with "victim" behaviors clearly indicates that it's time to adopt a more "warrior" attitude. A story that keeps defaulting back to the "princess" archetype can now shed light on why people don't like your spoiled, entitled personality.

Was there a key defining moment that sent you into depression, anxiety, worry, and fear? Did that event serve to change you from a "dreamer" to someone who never takes a risk or leaves their comfort zone?

If you are having trouble with this, go down the list of archetypes and ask yourself: "When did I first take on this way of being? What happened? Who was involved?" Perhaps the top troublesome archetype on your list is "fool." This can indicate not only a fool in love, but someone who has been hurt and betrayed for trusting others, putting faith in the wrong things and people, making mistakes and bad decisions, and even losing oneself to please another. Maybe as a child you had a father who was emotionally unavailable and you began to act like a "ham" to try to get his attention, practically throwing yourself at his feet to make him laugh and smile at your "foolish" antics. Pay attention to the words that pop up when you think back to these origin points of your behaviors because they are so telling and indicative.

"I first felt such a fool when I tried to sing a song for my dad and I forgot the words. He laughed at me and I was so embarrassed and hurt. I just wanted to please him."

Feeling a "fool" at that moment may have created additional situations where you had more opportunities to "play the fool," especially with men, in order to try to "please daddy" through them. It is all unconscious, unless you already know your patterns and are working to change them. But without going back to the first time you remember behaving or acting a certain way, it's hard to break the pattern. The child within will continue to act out that behavior unless we go that far back and reclaim ourselves in the moment.

Can we change the past? No. But we can reframe it and reclaim it. So you made a fool of yourself for your father's love and didn't succeed. Can you now see where your pattern of being the fool came from? Can you now reframe it to mean something else?

"My father couldn't express his love, but I know he cared about me. And even if he didn't, that has nothing to do with my worth as a human being or a woman. I don't have to throw myself at men and be a fool for their love. I am worthy of love and deserving of respect and acknowledgment. If I don't get that from a man, I walk away. I am not a fool anymore. I am a goddess!"

Now it's one thing to just say this, you have to believe it. And chances are a few more opportunities to play the fool will test you along the way, usually in relationships with the same gender of your father or the person who first hurt you. But the hardest and first step is becoming aware. The more you practice this and act "as if," the more the new archetype becomes embedded into your subconscious and your collective unconscious. Persistence is the key.

An Interview With Filmmaker Nicole Jones-Dion

Filmmakers work with visual images and stories to create movies that are meant to both entertain and give some insight into the human condition. Nicole Jones-Dion is an L.A.-based writer-director who specializes in genre films. Her credits include *Stasis*, from the executive producers of *Cloud Atlas*; *They Found Hell* for the SyFy Channel; *Dracula: The Dark Prince*, starring Academy Award–winner Jon Voight; and *Tekken 2: Kazuya's Revenge*, based on the best-selling video game series. She has several projects in development with Sean Cunningham, creator of *Friday the 13th*.

How do archetypes play a role in the work you have chosen to do?

I use archetypes all the time when I am creating characters for my films. They help create the foundation for strong, larger-than-life characters that offer a form of "shorthand" to the audience. Audiences are instantly drawn to archetype characters because they feel comfortable and familiar. Over time, certain character types have become part of the zeitgeist—like the loveable rogue or the reluctant messiah, the damsel in distress or the girl next door. While some archetypes may be considered culturally dependent, there are others that are universal, and those are the ones I tend to work with.

As a writer, these archetypes provide a canvas that can then be embellished with unique traits and quirks to help them stand out on their own as fully realized characters. Archetypes are universal in that they can be applied to both heroes and villains.

Do you think understanding and changing the archetypes that are actively influencing us can help us live a better life? Why?

Archetypes in fiction are one thing, but when you start to apply them to real people, problems can arise. We've been seeing this a lot lately in politics, where negative archetypes are being assigned to anyone we disagree with. While this is an effective means of propaganda because it bypasses the need for nuance or critical thinking, it can also be harmful because real people are complex with multiple layers and infinite shades of gray. To try to paint them with a broad brush can be misleading at best and incredibly damaging at worst.

Archetypes can be a powerful tool and should be treated accordingly.

How can the world at large benefit from understanding global archetypes, and do you believe they can be changed for a better world?

I think archetypes give us the tools to process a great deal of information very quickly. Once you start digging deeper, you might find that some perceptions of certain details within the archetypes may vary, but in general, most people see archetypes in more or less the same way. They provide us with a very powerful common language that transcends age, class, religion, and gender.

Working With "Parts" in Guided Meditation

Sometimes we need a little guidance to change our unwanted parts. This is where things like guided meditation and self-hypnosis can be wonderful tools. Guided meditation or visualization gives us a template to just relax and follow, taking some of the hard work off our shoulders. But we still have to do the visualizing! There are hundreds of products out there one can buy or download onto cell phones and tablets. Or you can record your own voice and play it back while meditating if you want to write your own guided journey.

Karey Keith is the force behind Majestic Insights (*www. majesticinsights.com*). She is an intuitive and psychic who works specifically with "parts" of the psyche to help empower, alter, or change them. Working with our "parts," which can be our archetypal patterns and identities, we can learn to clear out old habits, behavioral patterns, and even illnesses associated with that part. We can change our parts to make them function better. This applies both intensive hypnotherapy and guided meditation, but we can do this on our own in the comfort of our home to quickly change the energy pattern of our soul and change the archetype in question.

Karey does these sessions as part of her intuitive healing practice. She is also a coach and healer and can bring about fast changes that empower you to own your parts, manage them better, and stop those parts from being at cross-purposes. She gives the example of the "rebel" archetype, or part, which can get you into a lot of trouble with anti-social, rebellious behaviors such as smoking, drinking too much, fighting with others, and even violence. But by going within during a session, you can transform that rebel part of you into someone who instead challenges authority and expresses different opinions and attitudes in a more productive way.

Karey says, "You cannot cast out a part of yourself, but you can renegotiate them or reset them." Take your "judge," for instance; instead of always harshly judging yourself, you can make the judge the part of you that uses discernment and intuition when meeting someone new or getting into a new situation. Though working with an expert will lead to possibly deeper realizations and success, it is possible to do guided meditations and visualizations at home.

The following is a home exercise that you can either memorize or tape with your own voice and follow along. It can be done as many times as needed to change a part, but be careful to take a little time between sessions to recover and process what you've learned.

Meeting and Changing Your Parts: A Guided Meditation by Karey Keith

Find a quiet place and get into a relaxed state, eyes closed, breathing deeply into the lungs. Take your mind deeper into relaxation. Breathe.

Visualize a staircase. There are 10 steps. As you go up or down the steps, whichever you choose, you go deeper into yourself, more relaxed. Count down from 10 to 1.

Upon reaching 1, you are now in a sacred place, safe and protected. This can be a garden, by the sea, in the woods, or any place you visualize that feels like it is yours. You should now be experiencing Theta brainwaves, deeply relaxed.

Look around your sacred space. Take in the beauty, the sounds, and smells. Breathe the fresh air. If indoors, notice your surroundings, the fine details. Find a place to sit and relax deeper.

Notice if you are alone. If there is a person or animal there, ask if they are your guides. If they say no, let them run off. Ask for your spirit guide to come forth and be known. Once this happens, ask your spirit guide for a name (even if it is an animal!) and ask them to sit with you.

Ask your guide to show you the part of yourself that most needs to be healed, rebalanced, or renegotiated. Once that is revealed, visualize that part as a person, perhaps you as a child, or a teenager, or a young man or woman. When did this part first become a problem? That is the age you visualize into form.

Let the part manifest as a being you can speak to. Sit with the part of yourself and talk with it. Find out what happened to it that caused it to break off from the rest of you. Spend as much time as needed, but do know you can return to your sacred space numerous times to talk. If your part tells you anything, ask how you can help create a new and stronger perception. Take that part of you into your arms and love it.

If the part can be redeemed, you can allow it to stay in your sacred space. But if that part simply has outgrown its purpose and help to you, lovingly send it on its way, thanking it for what it has taught you. In your sacred space, there is no anger or resentment toward the part, so let go of it with love even if it caused you harm. Forgive it and move your attention back to your sacred space.

If you can redeem the part into something more empowering and beneficial, then you can walk with that part of you awhile, and get to know what it feels like. Then, embrace it into yourself and return up the 10 steps, this time counting from 1 to 10, and upon

9 open your eyes to come back to the normal waking state.

Do not question or second guess the information you received; rather, spend a few days allowing toxic energies that may have been raised to leave your body. It takes a few days to process this information and incorporate it, but as you do this, you can imagine that renegotiated part of you as being beside you as you go about your life. Make it a part of you in the now.

Return to the sacred place to work with additional parts once you feel you have integrated and processed the previous session.

Drink a lot of water and eat healthy to offset feeling weak or "off."

One of the benefits of this home exercise is the ability to also go into that sacred space and visualize someone important in your life you want to talk to on a soul level. Perhaps you have a family member or a lover you are having conflict with. You can call them into the sacred space with you. If they accept, you can discuss the issue with them on a deep, soulful level, and even ask them questions and listen for answers. The person will know on a soul level they are being communicated with, even if they have no conscious idea you are doing this exercise. This can be a powerful form of communication that bypasses the obstacles of the mind and brain.

Role Modeling

Who is living the kind of life you wish you were? Who has the kind of love, happiness, and success you dream of having? Who lights up the room and gives off a positive, powerful "vibe" when you are in their presence? These people are no better or luckier than any of the rest of us. They are just being something we can't, or haven't been able to be, up to this point: authentic. That is why we look at them and think, "I want what he/she is having!"

By role modeling, we can find tools and techniques to help us navigate the points in our story that someone else wrote in when we were asleep at the wheel or the pen. Granted, not everyone leads a perfect life, but we all know others who have so much love, light, and energy, who experience joy and abundance, and are passionate about their lives. We can find out what worked for them and try it ourselves. We can use them as a template for what we want to be like, while also recognizing our own uniqueness.

One thing about happy people is they are always willing to share their "horror stories" and how they turned them into "success stories." Ask them. They will be flattered and it gives them a chance to help others by telling their own life stories, warts and all. Needless to say, as they do, listen for the "aha" moments and discoveries that led them to realize they had to let go of the expectations and demands of others. Look for the ways they stood up against those who sought to tell them how to live. Identify the tools they used to ward off attempts to shape them into something they knew in their hearts they were not.

Then put these to use as you work with your own story, because all the knowledge and insight in the world is useless unless you put it into action. We will discuss tools in the next chapters. These role models are your "guardian angels," "mentors," "wizards," "sages," and "visionaries." Let them express their archetypes in a way that can help you. It's what they do!

Finding ways to reframe the past are wonderful tools for healing and growth, but we first have to own up to the past and tell our stories. And the way we remember them is critical. We cannot move forward to work with the archetypes that make up our stories, though, until we sit down and map out the past. However, some people, especially those who have experienced abuse of any kind, may want to work with a therapist or psychologist as these exercises can trigger traumatic emotions from reliving certain experiences without properly knowing how to fully process and work through them.

For those who feel ready to delve into the past, again, a sense of detached objectivity is a great way to get the key events on paper, which can then be examined in a more emotional light. But get them down on paper first. Leave no stone unturned, because sometimes the keys to rewriting the story and restructuring the foundation of who we are hide in the strangest of places, such as under rocks, in cracks, and crevices, not wanting to see the light of day. Dig those suckers out.

Get the timeline down, either from beginning to end or end to beginning, and star key defining moments, events, and circumstances that feel, on a gut level, like they shaped and molded you into something other than what you thought you wanted to be. Relive childhood dreams and desires for clues to who you were on the verge of becoming before the world created you in its own image. Not every childhood passion is meant to be carried into adulthood, but they often give us great food for thought as to what was important to us before we let others tell us otherwise.

Even examining old relationships that did not work can give great insight into what we want in a real relationship today and why we haven't found it yet. Are you tired of always running into "betrayers," "fools," and "villains"? We can identify our part in attracting these archetypal others so we can learn how to draw in the "lovers," "kings," "queens," "knights," "warriors," and "twin flames." These examinations may come with some pain and suffering as old wounds are reopened, but if the wounds can be reopened that easily, then we never healed them to begin with and they are still affecting us today in conscious and unconscious ways. We also get to find out when and where we became the "villains," "fools," and "betrayers" of our own authenticity, and were responsible for derailing our own lives off their destined paths.

Ultimately, we are responsible for quite a lot of our story, because even though we might have had false beliefs imposed upon us as children, now as adults we are capable of throwing those beliefs away if we have the insight and the courage. Too many people continue to go along with the status quo, never feeling too much in pain to change, but never feeling real happiness either. Our comfort zones are so deceptively soothing that they keep us trapped in mediocrity and unease. If we are lucky, we get a nice two-by-four to the head from the Universe/God/Life in the form of a wake-up call that shakes our very foundation and moves us toward changes we should have made a long time ago.

Sadly, many people ignore the two-by-fours until they are so powerful that they end up with a devastating illness or loss. Or they stay in denial until the day they die, filled with regrets about "what could have been." Life is always doling out those two-by-fours and if we are honest about reviewing our life stories, no doubt there will be numerous times we felt them but just kept doing what we were doing and hoping for a different result each time. That, by the way, is the definition of insanity!

An Interview With Atherton Drenth

Atherton Drenth is the author of *The Intuitive Dance: Building, Protecting & Clearing Your Energy* (Llewellyn Worldwide) and *Following Body Wisdom.* Atherton also appears in the documentary *Voyage to*

Betterment as one of 12 experts along with other internationally renowned physicians, researchers, and pioneers in the fields of consciousness research and spirituality. Atherton is a clairvoyant, medical intuitive, and holistic energy practitioner, facilitating transformational healing for her clients. She is also a compassionate teacher committed to helping others develop their full intuitive potential through yearly workshops. Her website is *www.athertondrenth.com.*

How do archetypes play a role in the work you have chosen to do?

As a clairvoyant medical intuitive and holistic energy practitioner, I work with clients to assist them on their healing journey. This means that we are focused on a client's overall health and well-being. We know that if a person's energy field is blocked, it can create problems physically, emotionally, mentally, and spiritually. I work with the client to find where their energy field is blocked and then we work together to release the block so that the body can continue its own healing journey. As a result, I have often found that clients fall into one of the following archetypes: victim, martyr, savior/servant. Understanding what archetype a client is subconsciously identifying with helps them to relate to where they are stuck in their emotional healing journey. We then work together to shift that belief. This empowers them to recognize that they have choices in how they respond to events in their lives.

The victim has a hard time accepting the fact that they have a choice in how they respond to abuse, for example. But once they do, they are empowered and quickly move through resolving the abuse, whether it is finally being able to overcome the memories from a tormented childhood or to leave a current abusive situation. This is often found in the physical/emotional fields.

The martyr believes that they need to carry the painful memories or stay in an abusive situation in order for others to survive. The parent who believes they need to stay for the children. The mother who chooses to live with an abuser because a child needs a father. The child who continues to live with an abusive parent because they have no one else to care for them. There is often a karmic connection here that takes time to uncover and resolve. This is often found in the mental/spiritual fields.

The savior/servant is confused about what it means to be of service. They give endlessly and then are afraid to receive. This is the person who volunteers for everything and can't accept a compliment or refuses any offer of assistance. They feel used, yet are afraid to turn down any request for help, thereby becoming a servant to others' needs regardless of what they have the time and energy for. They are often very spiritual or have a strong religious background. This block is usually found in the spiritual layer of their energy field.

Do you think understanding and changing the archetypes that are actively influencing us can help us live a better life? Why?

Understanding the archetypes can be useful so long as one realizes that they can choose what they identify with and that they have the power to make healthier emotional choices.

Can you give an example of how understanding and using archetypes has improved your own life? Or maybe a client story you would like to share?

As I worked through my own healing work, I found that I had moved through all of these archetypes at one time or another. Knowing and understanding how the archetypes operated made me more aware of how I was responding in different situations. Once I identified with what archetype I was in, it made easier for me to shift out and make a healthier, more balanced choice. That clarity and awareness, for me, was empowering.

The most dramatic example of how using archetypes can help in a client's session is when they are dealing with what I term *emotional blackmail*. This is a form of emotional bullying that uses any statement or accusation to undermine, challenge, or dismiss a person's feelings as being untrue and not believable. It is a form of emotional manipulation and sabotage that strikes at the heart of one's fears of being unlovable, isolated, and powerless. It makes a client afraid to defend themselves because deep down they are ultimately afraid that what the other person is saying is true. The abuser's ego has found a way to disempower the client's ego (see *The Intuitive Dance*, Chapter 10, page 163). A client who is subjected to emotional blackmail finds themselves instantly snapping into victim mode. Once a client identifies with the pattern, they are very open to learning how to create stronger emotional boundaries and not react to the emotional blackmail. It is one of the hardest forms of emotional abuse to overcome, in my professional experience, as it threatens one of greatest primal fears—isolation from the family tribe.

How can the world at large benefit from understanding global archetypes and do you believe they can be changed for a better world?

Personally, I think we need to acknowledge and incorporate the importance of the global archetypes of the divine mother and divine father. We need both working together. I think that the time has come to begin to incorporate that wisdom of the divine if we truly want to create a world of peace, love, and harmony.

Watch What You Say!

Dawn Romeo, author of *Change Your Story, Change Your Life* and a psychotherapist and coach, suggests focusing on the words and internal images, rather than the external circumstances. "The way we feel and the images we hold in the forefront of our mind manifests in the life we live. If you define yourself as a struggling single mother who barely makes enough money to survive, then this will continue to be your reality," she writes. Romeo emphasizes that how we define ourselves can shift our external circumstances and opportunities. What we focus on expands, so it behooves us to focus on the things we want, rather than what we do not want more of!

Romeo's book includes a seven-step plan for becoming the person we want to become, but it starts by first looking at who we are and where we are at in the present: "When you accept who you are in the present moment, then you can begin to change. You cannot change what you do not acknowledge." If we did the work first of getting our stories down and seeing how it all led up to who and where we are today, we can then move forward and begin to become the person we always envisioned ourselves to be. That word "envision" holds a lot of importance, because it signifies our "visual image" of the authentic, real self we somehow abandoned, lost, or replaced a long, long time ago.[1]

Authenticity comes when our image of who we want to be on the inside matches our outside projection and the way we portray ourselves to others.

An Interview With Amy Leigh Mercree

Amy Leigh Mercree's motto is "Live joy. Be kind. Love unconditionally." She counsels women and men in the underrated art of self-love to create happier lives. Mercree is an author, media personality, and medical intuitive. She speaks internationally, focusing on kindness, joy, and wellness.

Mercree is the best-selling author of *The Spiritual Girl's Guide to Dating: Your Enlightened Path to Love, Sex, and Soul Mates*; *A Little Bit of Chakras: An Introduction to Energy Healing*; *Joyful Living: 101 Ways to Transform Your Spirit and Revitalize Your Life*; *The Chakras and Crystals Cookbook: Juices, Sorbets, Smoothies, Salads, and Crystal Infusions to Empower Your Energy Centers*; and *The Compassion Revolution: 30 Days of Living from the Heart*.

How do archetypes play a role in the work you have chosen to do?

Sometimes people have archetypal roles that they are playing out in their lives that they're not aware of. These can cause mental and emotional imbalances as well as spiritual imbalances. In some cases, they can also cause physical ailments. In those cases, as those energetic imbalances are addressed, then people are able to clear denser energies from their body or energies that are stuck. Clearing dense or stuck energy from the body raises our vibration, which improves our health and our quality of life.

Do you think understanding and changing the archetypes that are actively influencing us can help us live a better life? Why?

I think they absolutely can. If we are playing out an old script, whether it is from our family of origin, ancestors, or the archetypal influences of humanity, then we are not living as consciously as we could be. The more awareness we bring to why we do what we do, the more of a conscious life we can live. A conscious life is a happy life. A conscious life is a life in which we understand the energy that is in play and feel peaceful with what happens.

The Power of Complaining

One of the best ways to identify archetypes at work in your life that you want to change is to write down your complaints as they pop up throughout your day. Do you find yourself whining and moaning about the same things? Do you get together with friends and complain or hold "bitch sessions"? By acknowledging the things you bitch about all the time, you open a treasure chest of potential gifts for transformation and change.

Make a list:

I am sick of _____.

I am so tired of _____.

I can't take _____ anymore.

I don't understand why_____.

I wish _____.

I have had enough of people who_____.

I can't take _____ anymore.

Why don't people stop _____?

Why can't I _____?

Looking at complaints can help target patterns that need to be addressed and symbolic beliefs that need to be changed! What we complain about are the things that are keeping us from a happy, authentic expression of who we are. What we moan and groan about, whether it is our health, lack of funds, lousy boss, crappy job, mean relatives, jiggly thighs, or horrid dating prospects, indicates what isn't working. If we continuously complain about the same things, we have an ingrown pattern that must be addressed. Often at the root of those patterns are the archetypes we are still operating from.

Example 1: You complain for years about how your boss takes advantage of you, and also how the men you've been dating treat you no better. Are you stuck in your "victim" archetype?

What would happen if you decided to take on the aspects of "warrior" or "queen" instead? By choosing those symbols rather than the disempowering one of "victim," imagine now how a warrior queen would act if her boss mistreated her. Imagine how she would behave if the man she was dating took her for granted. Then act on that, because the truth is that nothing more has to happen for someone to become a warrior queen (or king) than to desire to become one!

Changing behaviors once is not enough, though. Focused, consistent action, acting "as if," will lead to new archetypes embedding themselves in the collective unconscious. Soon, the old pattern and symbols are replaced with the newer, more effective model and external situations begin to change because of it. So within, so without.

Example 2: You complain many times a day that you are sick and tired of this or that, and then complain you are always sick and tired. Are you stuck in a "sickly person" archetype?

What if you saw yourself as healing and powerful, filled with good health, vibrant, and passionate about life? Would you carry yourself differently if you could become a "god" or "goddess" instead? Gods and goddesses don't complain about being sick and tired, because they are more powerful than illness and exhaustion. They do their best to never fall into either state of health or, if they do, they take good care of themselves and they don't feel selfish for it. How about rethinking yourself as "athlete" or "superhero"? You don't have to run a marathon or don a cape, but by showing gratitude for your body and focusing more on how well it operates without having to control it (instead of what you don't like about it), you automatically create the foundation to make it stronger and healthier.

The things we say to ourselves when we whine can be so telling as to what we need to change! Try tracking your complaints for a few days by writing them down as you express them and look for the patterns and symbols hidden within. If the majority of the words coming out of your mouth are negative and you are constantly reinforcing archetypes you don't like or want, you will just get more of what you don't want. Why? *Because that is what you are focusing on!*

Instead, turn your focus toward the image and vision of who you feel you truly are and begin expressing from that vision, even if you have to fake it until you make it.

Example 3: You complain incessantly about how people around you won't do as you say, and how you know what is best for them, if only they'd listen. They refuse to acknowledge your experience and ignore your suggestions for how they can do things better. Are you stuck in "tyrant" mode?

How different would people around you respond if you instead took on "visionary" or "guide"? Instead of lecturing and judging everyone, what if you could provide them with the vision, direction, and insight as to how to achieve it? Even better, what if you offered to be more of a "mentor" and less of a "dictator"? Would they respond better and be more open to your ideas and suggestions? I bet they would indeed.

Swapping out the negative for the positive is easy once you own up to the negatives you've been operating by. One of the biggest problems is getting out of denial and being honest about this. It may be a blow to your ego or cause some shame and embarrassment, but that is a small price to pay for truly transforming yourself and your life into something wonderfully authentic.

Chakras as Archetypes

The body has seven energy wheels called "chakras," which comes from the Sanskrit word *chakra*. These seven energy wheels are located at various points on the body and contain bundles of nerves and vital organs. They also align with our psychological, emotional, and spiritual states of being according to Michelle Fondin in her article "What Is a Chakra?" for The Chopra Center.[2] The chakras are a major part of meditation, yogic and Ayurvedic practices in the East, and now also in the West where they are incorporated into the spiritual practices of those seeking to balance, harmonize, and correct bodily energies.

There are seven chakras, each one archetypal in and of itself. But they also correspond with archetypes that can be worked with to create the desired physical and psychological outcome.

The first chakra, the Muladhara, represents our basic needs and stability. It is located at the base of the spine and the colon area. It is called the "root" chakra and it corresponds to the mother and father archetypes in the positive, and the victim and martyr in the negative. The balance must occur between our need to survive and be secure, and our need to nourish, be in harmony with life, and mother or father ourselves back to love.

The second chakra, Svadhisthana, is the sacral energy center of sexual well-being and creativity. It is located at the pubic bone below the belly button. The corresponding archetypes are king/queen and emperor/empress in the positive, and martyr in the negative. Balancing our worldly desires and pleasure seeking with our penchant for suffering and playing victim is the role of this happiness-oriented chakra.

The third chakra, Manipura, is the energy area between the belly button and the breastbone, known as the solar plexus, and the source of our confidence, self-worth, and personal power. In the positive, it is the warrior archetype; in the negative, it is the servant.

The fourth chakra is Anahata, the heart area, and corresponds to love, joy, peace, and unity with life and others. In the positive, the archetype is the free-spirited, generous lover. In the negative, it is the actor wearing a mask and covering hidden agendas and motives.

The fifth chakra is Vishuddha, also called the throat chakra. Through this energy center we speak our highest truths and verbalize our expression. The positive archetypes are communicator/leader and the negative are the child (often voiceless) and innocent. The balance occurs when we find our voice and speak it.

The sixth chakra is Ajna, associated with the "third eye" area of the forehead between the eyes. This chakra is where our intuition, imagination, and wisdom originate. The positive archetype is psychic/wise sage/intuitive and the negative is intellectual/rationalist. We must be a balance of both the intuitive and the rational.

The seventh chakra is Sahaswara, located at the crown, on top of the head. This chakra is all about enlightenment and connecting to our higher self and sources of wisdom. The positive archetype is guru/teacher/mentor, and the negative is egotist/narcissist. To reach enlightenment, we must release the attachments of ego.

The chakras represent deep energies, behaviors, and emotions that must be brought into balance to achieve true well-being.

Working With Chakra Archetypes

Shelly Wilson is an author, intuitive medium, and conscious creator who is passionate about helping people wake up to their greatness. She supports others as they navigate their own journey into consciousness. Shelly's books, *28 Days to a New YOU*, *Connect to the YOU Within*, and *Journey into Consciousness*, are available in paperback and e-book format. Her websites are *http://shellyrwilson.com* and *http://facebook.com/intuitivemediumshelly*.

Strengthen Your Chakras With Visualization by Shelly Wilson

Maintaining a healthy and balanced chakra system is essential. Allow yourself the opportunity to tune in to what your physical body and energetic centers are conveying to you. In addition to clearing and balancing your chakras, it is important and beneficial to *strengthen* them as well through intention and visualization involving color.

Using the respective color for each chakra, set the intention to first clear, balance, and then strengthen each one. To begin with, focus on bringing your energy to the present moment in the here and now. Then, set the intention to ground and center your energy by envisioning your legs as tree roots growing deep into the earth (grounding) and a ball of white light at your core (centering). Take a big deep breath and visualize yourself breathing in emerald green healing energy and letting go of anyone and anything that no longer serves you or your highest purpose, including any fear, worry, doubt, or any of the lower vibrational emotions. Consciously choose to feel these emotions, so that you can acknowledge and release them as you move into the higher vibrational heart-space of love and trust.

The root or base chakra is red and is associated with survival needs along with the lower vibrational energies of worry, fear, doubt, regret, guilt, and shame. It is our foundation and the connection to the physical plane. Physical organs include the colon, rectum, and adrenal glands. To balance and strengthen this energy center, *work with the color red for the root chakra* and with red crystals, such as jasper, garnet, or any of the grounding crystals, including hematite, smoky quartz, or jet.

The sacral chakra is orange and is correlated with creativity, inspiration, and sexuality. Physical organs include the kidneys, lower abdomen, liver, prostate gland, and reproductive systems. To balance and strengthen this energy center, *work with the color orange for the sacral chakra* and with orange crystals, such as carnelian, topaz, and orange calcite.

The solar plexus chakra is yellow and is your power center and *gut* instinct. The digestive system, spleen, and stomach are the physical organs connected to the solar plexus, which is related to our will, personal power, and identity. To balance and strengthen this energy center, *work with the color yellow for the solar plexus chakra* and with yellow crystals, such as citrine, yellow calcite, yellow tourmaline, and tiger's eye.

The heart chakra is green and is associated with love, including love for self and others, and all other emotions. Our *spiritual home*, the heart chakra is tied to the physical body organs of the heart, lungs, rib cage, thymus gland, and breasts. To balance and strengthen this energy center, *work with the color green for the heart chakra* and with green crystals, such as amazonite, aventurine, and chrysoprase, as well as pink rose quartz, which is the stone of unconditional love.

The throat chakra is blue and is your voice—the area of communication and self-expression. Physical body organs involve the neck, voice, thyroid gland, and throat. To balance and strengthen this energy center, *work with the color blue for the throat chakra* and with blue crystals, such as blue lace agate, blue calcite, lapis lazuli, and sodalite.

The third eye chakra is indigo or violet in color and is your area of intuition and spiritual awareness. The physical body organs include the pituitary gland and the higher brain centers, including the endocrine and nervous systems. To balance and strengthen this energy center, *work with the color purple for the third eye chakra* and with purple crystals, such as amethyst and purple fluorite.

The crown chakra is white and is your connection to Source energy. This energy center involves all-knowing and understanding and is connected to the pineal gland and highest brain centers, including metabolism. To balance and strengthen this energy center, *work with the color white for the crown chakra* and with clear crystals, such as crystal quartz, clear tourmaline, and opal.

Balancing Act

Imagine a scale with bricks on one side and a single feather on the other. Would this scale be considered balanced? Not by a long shot. Yet how often do we go through life with imbalanced aspects making us feel off-balance and out of harmony with our own integrity and values?

As we look closer and closer at what archetypes operate in our lives, we often see these imbalances and begin to realize how they have been making things much harder for us. To not have inner harmony and balance is to walk through the world without a sense of being centered, grounded, and at peace. We don't feel authentic at all, but rather experience a sort of mental "vertigo" that pulls us in one direction, even when we wish to go in another.

What causes this sense of vertigo? When one archetype has way more power over us than it should, we experience the results as chaos, discord, and lack of alignment between what we truly want and what we keep doing again and again with the same results. By recognizing which archetypes are out of balance and need adjusting, we can begin experiencing a stronger inner peace and personal power because the scales are more even and so, too, are we.

Example: You are always angry at everyone. You always have to be right or you feel as though your entire identity is shattered and you no longer exist. You are bitter at the world and everyone who ever did you wrong. You are never at peace and always in an argument with someone over something.

Your angry "dictator" is out of control here.

Try this: Using whatever tool works best, visualizing, meditating, or journaling, get into that sacred space where you can call up the "dictator." See that aspect of you standing on one side of your scales, making it grossly uneven. Tell it that unless it calms down, you will have to send it packing.

Now, call into your space the "diplomat," or any other archetypes that you feel would balance the negatives. See that aspect step on the opposite side of the scale, bringing it into balance. The "dictator" can serve you well at times when you do need to firmly tell others what to do, as in delegating at work or managing a large group of people, but now your "diplomat" will balance out the anger and forcefulness, and provide you with a more even-keeled ability to instruct others to do what you want and need them to do.

Another example: Your ego is getting a bit out of control. Friends say you are acting like a diva and a bitch. You talk to others condescendingly and often leave people wanting to run away from you as fast as they can. Men think you are cold and haughty. Nobody likes you, Miss Thang!

Your "queen" needs her comeuppance!

Try this: Go into your space and call up the "queen" in you (or "king" as the case may be). Tell her to sit down and shut up. You have something to say. Imagine her sitting on one side of the giant scale in your mind and, wow, is she tipping the scales. It's as if she weighs a ton, and she does, but it's all her ego!

Now call in your "mother" and ask her to sit down on the other side of the scale. Watch how her loving and nurturing energy balances the scales. You do want to be a "queen," but one that is powerful and caring, influential and friendly, warm and inviting yet also full of a solid sense of self-worth and appreciation. The "mother" balances the "queen" so that you can express both now in a much more positive fashion and become more of a loving leader than a stuck-up royal snob.

We may not always want to eliminate archetypes even if they are out of balance, because some of their traits are helpful and positive at the appropriate times. By balancing the scales, we can make sure that there is a sense of real harmony within and, therefore, in our external world because we don't feel so "one-sided" or extreme in our thoughts, actions, and behaviors.

If your "rebel" is acting out in harmful ways, you can even invite that aspect to "balance itself out" on the scales by finding a new way for this archetype to express rebellion and defiance. Instead of acting out in violent or abusive ways, or acting from a place of anger, rage, or revenge, bringing the positive "rebel" onto the scale can balance that particular archetype in the same fashion, without having to actually replace it. You may love to be a "rebel," but you want to be one that doesn't end up doing harm to the self or to others. Balance those extremes!

In *Goddesses in Everywoman: Powerful Archetypes in Women's Lives*, Jean Shinoda Bolen breaks down the goddesses of mythology into symbols of different aspects of women's lives. The same could be done with gods, by the way, as the pantheon of myth is filled with wonderful archetypes, both female and male. Bolen examines:

Artemis: Goddess of the hunt, independent and achievement-oriented.

Athena: Goddess of wisdom, logical, self-assured, and ruled by the head, not heart.

Hestia: Goddess of the hearth, patient and steady, intact and whole.

Hera: Goddess of marriage, a wife to a husband before she is anything else.

Demeter: Goddess of grain and the maternal, nurturing to her children.

Persephone: Goddess of the underworld, a maiden who is passive and wants to please others.

Aphrodite: Goddess of love, beauty, sexuality, and sensuality.[3]

Mythical deities are archetypal because they were purposely written to have universal appeal and influence us on a deep psychological level. By taking on aspects of a particular god or goddess, we can decide then whether they work for or against us, and possibly trade them out for a new way of looking at ourselves. Too much Hera might leave a woman feeling like a "martyr" or "victim," so she may want to nurture the Aphrodite in her.

Likewise, a woman expressing too much sexuality of Aphrodite may find herself wanting to become more nurturing and even find one man she can be with for the rest of her life. She needs then to work with her Hera and Hestia and balance the extremes out.

For men, is there perhaps too much of the angry, dictatorial Zeus? Never having any fun? Maybe it's time for a little Dionysus and his decadent, life-loving ways! Or maybe a man wishes to be more of a Loki trickster and make some innocent mischief instead of always being so serious.

By ascribing mythological figures to the personality traits and aspects of the self we want to work on, it actually helps clarify what we need to change that we may not readily identify in ourselves, but can easily see in the deity we have an affinity with. Bolen writes, "Just as women used to be unconscious of the powerful effects that cultural stereotypes had on them, they may also be unconscious of the powerful forces within them that influence what they do and how they feel." Bolen's book and her other works teach women to look at those influences and reshape them in order to also reshape her unfolding life story.

Bolen examines the many ways goddesses are "activated" within women at different times of their lives. From inherent predispositions women are born into the world with, to hormonal shifts and changes, and family environments, different goddesses are put into play in a woman's life with varying results. Other activating circumstances include coming into contact with certain people and events that trigger the goddesses to show up, as well as when a woman begins "doing," which "expresses a way that goddesses can be evoked or developed by a chosen course of action."[4]

Obviously, as a woman goes through the different life stages of puberty, young adulthood, adulthood, middle age, menopause, and old age, the goddesses that are activated change and morph and some may stop being activated altogether. The maiden goddesses will eventually give way to the mother aspects, which in turn give way to the crone aspects of old age.

Again, the phases and stages of a man's life activate different gods as a boy becomes a young man, goes into the world as an adult, through midlife (often accompanied by some kind of existential crisis!), and then the senior years. Old gods give way to the new and some stick around for the duration of a lifetime, even as they take a backseat to the newer for the sake of growth and evolution.

If taking on the personas of gods and goddesses doesn't turn you on, try giving your different aspects names: the whiny, negative Nancy; the bold and bodacious Lola; the brave and courageous Leo; or the quiet and studious George. It's almost like having multiple personalities, yet our main personality is always in control in this case. But having fun with these processes makes you want to actually do them, so play with it. Let your inner Clyde out, or your inner Cleo!

Giving something a name is a powerful thing, though, because names themselves can become symbolic of certain aspects of behavior. Look at pop culture, for example. A Marilyn is thought to be someone sexy and feminine, like Marilyn Monroe. A Betty is a gorgeous woman, a la Betty Grable. A Samson is big and strong, like Samson in the Old Testament. A Noah is usually an animal lover, like Noah and his Ark! Chad is a collegiate type. Susan is the girl next door. John and Jane are the everyman and everywoman. So naming our parts is a great way to tag them with the archetypal traits we most identify with.

The Aborigines of Australasia believed that naming something is what gave it a particular power. In their cosmogenesis, or origin story, they would walk around and sing something into being thus giving it an identity based upon the name they spoke. Words are critical to the origin of a thing, as we see in the Old Testament story of Genesis, when God speaks, and the Logos or *Word* of God creates light and then all of existence. But the word was first!

Act as If

Yes, let out the inner actor or actress, because acting as if is a great way to turn a desire into a reality. When we act as if we already have something, we take on all the qualities necessary to actually make it happen. Habitual behaviors are things we took on without much conscious awareness, allowing our subconscious and collective unconscious to program us without a fight. Now it's time to deprogram the deeper levels of the mind that are controlling us and telling us who we are and what we want, and replace those programs with images and words, thoughts and behaviors that work!

Prosperity teachers talk about getting out of a consciousness of lack by acting as if one was rich. By pretending to be rich and feeling what it would be like to prosper and have wealth, they say we begin to adopt the right thought patterns and behaviors that will lead us to opportunities and people who can help us become rich. This is the Law of Attraction at work, and although it may be more involved than just pretending, we certainly won't change our behaviors if we continue to buy into the belief we are poor and undeserving.

So it does make sense to put on our actor's hats, even activate the actor and actress archetypes within, to help us adopt and embed these new beliefs and behaviors and make them a part of our internal programming.

So how can we just pretend to be something when reality is showing us we are not that yet? It's not about the external, but the internal, where manifestation begins. When we get into the feeling of something, how it would feel to be wealthy, healthy, empowered, compassionate, bold, or anything else, we begin to incorporate that energy into our internal being, making it a part of us that will, when the tipping point is reached, tip the scales in favor of what we now desire. That tipping point comes from disciplined thought and action toward what we want, as opposed to what we don't want. It happens when we've felt our way into the new reality we want to experience.

For example: we want to be more "warrior" than "victim." When we awaken in the morning, we can do a quick and quiet visualization of what our day will be like if we approach everything as a "warrior." How might things turn out if we are bold, courageous, and willing to take on any challenge? How could we live differently if we leave the "victim" at home and let the "warrior" go into the world wearing a shield of love, compassion, honor, courage, and strength?

Throughout our day we can remind ourselves to get back into "warrior" mode if we slip back to default status. If we do this enough, eventually we won't even have to visualize in the morning because "warrior" will become our default mode of behavior and how we go into the world, act, and behave. We have now changed the programming operating in the deep mind by constantly and consistently acting "as if" we were a "warrior" and not a "victim."

Affirmations work wonderfully, too, for reprogramming our new archetypes into our personalities. Affirmations must be in the present tense, and must not focus on what we don't want or want to get rid of. It's pretty simple. Instead of saying I want to be a "warrior," "goddess," or "hero," we must say *I am a warrior, goddess, or hero. I am* should always be at the beginning of our affirmations because we are telling ourselves what we are, not asking or saying we "want" to be this or that, or even stating that we will someday in the future: *I am this now. I am that now. I react today from my inner queen. I rule my world as a compassionate king. I am the hero of my story. I am a loving mother nurturing the world. I am a courageous explorer. I am a visionary at my job.*

Remember that the subconscious mind, as well as the unconscious, is very susceptible to what we tell it with our words and thoughts. When we tell the subconscious continuously "I want to be..." all we get are more situations where we "want to be." If we constantly say "I will become..." then the world doles us back situations and circumstances where we always wish we would become... So we must be very careful to send the right messages to the lower levels of the mind. Saying "I am" is taken literally in the deep mind. Saying it again and again becomes the new "normal" mode of thought and behavior. Never give yourself more of what you don't want!

I am…

I do…

I have…

I experience…

I create…

I manifest…

Think of yourself as the ultimate "creator" archetype, and your words are the Logos from which all else in your life is manifested. Speak it as if it's already a done deal. Speak it into being! Or sing it if you wish.

There are a million books and websites devoted to affirmations, but as long as we keep it in the present tense and focused on the desired outcome as if it already exists, we don't need to spend a ton of money learning how to write and speak them. Affirmation cards put in strategic places around the home or office help remind us to declare our intention to the Source or God or Universe. We can command that the Source works for us, or against us, and the Source doesn't care either way. It works no matter what messages, orders, and intentions we give it.

One of the best concepts this author has ever come across for working with the Law of Attraction (LOA) is called Placing Your Order. The idea is you imagine the Universe is a big diner and you are sitting down to have a meal. The waiter hands you a menu and on that menu are an infinite number of choices you can make. Wow, pretty mind-blowing. So you pick what you want the most and tell the waiter. He takes down your order, goes into the back, and gives it to the kitchen staff to begin preparing.

Right at this point is where most people trip themselves up with working with the LOA. They don't "let go" and let the Universe make the damn food and serve it up! Instead, they call the waiter back and change the order or, out of fear and doubt, they cancel the order completely and go home and make a sandwich. What gives? The power of LOA and intention comes from being decisive, firm, commanding, and even demanding. You place your order and you wait in patience and faith for it to come. When it does, you feast. But too many of us stop this process cold because we are afraid it won't work, it seems to be taking so long, or we doubt we deserve our order in the first place.

No wonder we never get half the things we say we truly want. We're always cancelling the order before it ever leaves the kitchen and gets to our table.

Have faith. Be patient. Place the order. Wait nicely. Enjoy your meal!

[chapter 7]

Working With Guides, Symbols, and Dreams

Millions of people believe in angels and guardian spirits that are always available to offer us wisdom or guide us in the right direction. These entities are archetypes of their own kind as representative of the higher sources of wisdom we all have access to. We can call upon these entities anytime through rituals, prayer, or meditations. Perhaps our intuitive hunches and gut instincts come from this higher plane of wisdom, where all information can be accessed that our conscious minds don't always have access to. The whispers of God, the Universe, Life, Source, Spirit, or even just our own higher selves are the language of the archetypes giving us exactly what we need when we need it.

The problem is that we need to get quiet and still enough to listen to what they are saying. The patterns of our subconscious also speak to us, usually via kneejerk behaviors and reactions, and if we pay close attention, we can learn how to change the way we respond to situations. Kneejerk reactions are not of the higher level; they are not instinct or intuition, but instead base reactions that come from fear-based parts of the past.

Instinct, intuition, and the guidance we get from higher aspects of our own beings or other beings entirely are always beneficial to us. They serve to keep us out of danger, acknowledge red flags, move toward the deepest desires of the authentic self, and see the signs erected along the pathways that lead us to our destinies.

Archangels as Archetypes of Energy by Shelly Wilson

Religious connotations depict archangels as part of the celestial hierarchy. Their purpose is to carry God's message to humans and assist us as we go about our everyday lives. However, archangels can also be viewed as energetic archetypes with each individual archangel representing an archetype of energy that is accessible at any time. All one has to do is meditate on this energy and set the intention to work with it.

Archangels are not human and are therefore not male or female, although they have a masculine and feminine aspect. For reference purposes, many times they are viewed as a specific gender, which is what the pronoun usage denotes. These celestial beings, known as angels, continue to remind us that they are with us standing by ready, willing, and able to assist. All we have to do is ask for their assistance and set the intention to work with their energetic archetype, as they cannot intervene in our freewill choices unless the consequences are dire and it is not our time to depart the earthly plane. These archetypes have no linear time or space restrictions, so their energy is accessible to everyone at all times.

Most people are familiar with four of the archangels—Michael, Raphael, Gabriel, and Uriel. Archangel Michael is deemed a masculine energy and represents the energy of strength, courage, and protection. He is often observed as a blue energy and is the angel to invoke when determination is needed along with direction in life. Archangel Raphael is typically viewed as a green energy and denotes healing as well as physical and mental/emotional well-being. He is also connected to the heart chakra. Invoke Raphael to request healing energy for yourself and others as well as for animals.

Archangel Gabriel is the angel of communication and reminds us to speak our truth. This enables us to connect with our divine potential and to also realize it. Invoking the archetypal energy Gabriel represents while visualizing the color blue in the throat area assists with clearing, balancing, and strengthening the throat chakra. Archangel Uriel is the angel of knowledge who offers us inspiration and insight. This information comes into our awareness through the crown chakra. Invoke Uriel when you need help in achieving your full potential and to gain an increased understanding of who you are.

Additionally, Archangel Chamuel embodies the energy of love and peace and assists in finding anything that is lost, including objects and relationships.

Invoking the energy of Archangel Ariel supports mani-festing our heart's desire, while feeling empowered to do so. Archangel Metatron is an excellent choice to invoke when you need assistance with writing, and he will also help you to achieve your potential through prioritization. Archangel Azrael is the angel of both endings/death and beginnings/birth. He is also the ar-chetype of change and transition. Therefore, working with his comforting energy assists us as we navigate through the challenges and triumphs of life.

Archangel Jophiel is the angel of nature and beauty who helps us to see experiences from a higher soul per-spective. She exemplifies herself as a beautiful pink-colored energy and is perfect for clearing energetic and physical clutter from our life. Archangel Raguel aids us with resolving arguments and conflicts of all kinds. His archetypal energy represents harmony in relationships and encourages us to tap into our emotions. Archangel Haniel helps us to understand and work with the power of the moon cycles and assists with strengthening our psychic abilities by tuning into our sensitivity.

Please know that there are many others in addition to those listed here. You may be guided to seek credible resources to learn more about the archangels and how to access their energy.

Animal Guides and Astrological Symbols

Shamans use spirit guides on their journeys into the underworld and upperworld. These guides may be human, animal, or even the elements themselves. The natural world, to shamans, is filled with archetypes always ready to give their wisdom, strength, and healing properties as needed.

Native beliefs in spirit animals give archetypal qualities to specific animals that govern our lives based usually upon when we were born, similar to the signs of the Zodiac.

In astrology, 12 archetypal symbols are used to describe the signs ascribed to our birth months. We may not think about this when we check our daily horoscope to see if fortune will befall us, but these are ingrained into the collective unconscious whether we follow astrological teachings or not.

The 12 signs are:

Aries (March 21–April 19): The warrior, represented by Mars and the element of fire. Aries is charismatic, demanding, ambitious, and passionate. Aries is a leader, but can be a demanding and impetuous one.

Taurus (April 20–May 20): The bull, strong and often stubborn, persistent and hard-working, loyal and true. Represented by Venus and the fixed element of Earth, Taurus is patient, secure, and values home and family, but can be possessive.

Gemini (May 21–June 20): The planet Mercury and the element of air govern the Twins, who represent communication, change, intelligence, and multitasking, but can be indecisive, too. A Gemini is a great instructor and teacher who loves variety.

Cancer (June 21–July 22): This water sign is represented by the Moon; it's emotional and impulsive, but intense and diplomatic. Cancer is imaginative and intuitive, creative and sensual.

Leo (July 23–August 22): The fire sign represented by the Sun, Leo is the king and a natural leader. Warm, strong, full of his or herself, confident, and magnetic, Leo accomplishes much and takes pride in those accomplishments. Leos can be arrogant and haughty.

Virgo (August 23–September 22): A fixed Earth sign represented by the planet Mercury. Virgo is practical, analytical, and reflective. Virgos observe everything and can be overly critical. They have integrity and are good problem-solvers, but can get lost in fine details.

Libra (September 23–October 22): An air sign represented by the planet of love and beauty, Venus. Justice, equality, the balance of the "scales" of life, beauty, and aesthetics are important to this social butterfly and natural diplomat. But Libras can be very indecisive and waver back and forth between two choices.

Scorpio (October 23–November 21): The water sign of the planet Mars, Scorpios are purposeful, willful, and often won't give in to others. They can be passionate and even jealous, and are competitive, creative, and imaginative.

Sagittarius (November 22–December 21): The fire sign represented by Jupiter, this sign loves to philosophize, experiment, and be creative. Optimistic and honest, they love traveling and exploring the world.

Capricorn (December 22–January 19): The fixed Earth sign represented by Saturn, the Goat can be determined, persevering, solid, and hard-working. Practical and moral, this sign has trouble with change and seeing others' points of view.

Aquarius (January 20–February 18): An air sign of the planet Uranus, the knowledge-seekers and insightful thinkers of the Zodiac. They love a good debate, are wise, just, and idealistic. This sign can often seem too opinionated and unorthodox.

Pisces (February 19–March 20): A fluid water sign of the planet Neptune, Pisces has imagination and depth of character. They are deeply intuitive, highly artistic, and the dreamers of the Zodiac, but can be indecisive and unable to face reality.

The signs that we identify with often take on a sort of power of suggestion. This author is a Libra and is indeed a justice freak who cannot make a decision to save her life. Because the signs are so embedded in the collective unconscious, we often blame certain behavior patterns on them, just as we attribute the good traits to them. The interesting thing is that traditional Vedic astrology of the East bumps our sign back to the sign right before it. So this author goes from being a Libra to a Virgo in Vedic astrology. Virgos can make up their minds and may not care as much about fairness. So which sign influences the author more? Libra—simply because that is what she has "believed" herself to be most of her life!

Sometimes we take on our sign's characteristics just because we are told that is who we are according to the day and month of our birth. But there are aspects of each sign we fit and those we don't, just as there are aspects of any archetype that fit and those that don't. Our astrological signs can be a guide or a template of who we are, but they are not the fullness of our potential and, if we hate the fact that as a Libra we can't make decisions without extreme bouts of agony, it is something we can change. It's not something we are stuck with, like a dimple or giant ears.

Chinese astrology has become popular the world over recently, and provides us with archetypal traits that are based on the animal that represents the year we were born. Each of the 12 signs cycles like the Zodiac and offers particular characteristics for that sign. The signs come back into play every 12 years. Did we talk about the archetypal nature of numbers? Twelve is most certainly one we see again and again, all over the world, and usually in a sacred context.

Rat (1948, 1960, 1972, 1984, 1996, 2008, 2020): Those born in these years are said to be popular with others, very inventive, and artistic.

Ox (1949, 1961, 1973, 1985, 1997, 2009, 2021): The Ox is calm, strong, and dependable with great ideas.

Tiger (1950, 1962, 1974, 1986, 1998, 2010, 2022): Tigers are brave, deep thinkers, and courageous.

Rabbit (1939, 1951, 1963, 1975, 1987, 1999, 2011, 2023): Rabbits are kind, expressive, and trustworthy.

Dragon (1940, 1952, 1964, 1976, 1988, 2000, 2012, 2024): Dragons are energetic, good friends, and great listeners.

Snake (1941, 1953, 1965, 1977, 1989, 2001, 2013, 2025): The Snake is lucky with money and loves good food, books, and ideas.

Horse (1942, 1954, 1966, 1978, 1990, 2002, 2014, 2026): Horses are happy, hard-working, and popular.

Ram (1943, 1955, 1967, 1979, 1991, 2003, 2015, 2027): Rams like fine things, are artistic, and wise.

Monkey (1944, 1956, 1968, 1980, 1992, 2004, 2016, 2028): Monkeys are funny, fun-loving, and good at solving problems.

Rooster (1945, 1957, 1969, 1981, 1993, 2005, 2017, 2029): The Rooster is a hard-working and talented deep-thinker.

Dog (1946, 1958, 1970, 1982, 1994, 2006, 2018, 2030): Dogs are loyal, keep secrets well, and worry a lot.

Pig (1947, 1959, 1971, 1983, 1995, 2007, 2019, 2031): Pigs are studious, honest, and brave.

The Chinese collectively celebrate each year and believe that year will take on some of the traits of the sign itself, just as it does on a personal level. Each sign, just as in the Western Zodiac, has a positive and negative spin. For example, a Dog can be loyal, but perhaps to the extreme, which causes them to be victimized by others. A Monkey can spend too much time being funny and playing, and never get serious enough to hold down a job. An Ox can be too strong for others all the time, and then fall apart from lack of self-care. Balancing the characteristics of each sign is key.[1]

Native American traditions also have their own Zodiac of animal symbols. Many Native cultures believe that a person is assigned a particular spirit or power animal from birth, also called a totem, and that they take on the traits of that animal (good and bad).

Each Native American tribe has its own Zodiac of animal signs that are important to its mythology, geographical region, and experiences, so not all are the same. But our desire to associate ourselves with a "symbol" or sign, animal or otherwise, is a strong and universal one. It also shows our deep-seated respect and reverence for the natural world around us, and a strong belief that the day and month of our birth is important, even archetypal, and thus requires a system like the Zodiac to chart out the characteristics of each sign's positive and negative aspects.

For example, Wolf can be courageous, family-oriented, fierce, loyal, and bold; but a Wolf can also be isolated, too fierce, vicious, hostile, and predatory. Hawk can have incredible vision and foresight, but might also be a bit of a judge and critic from its haughty position above the ground. Deer can be sweet, witty, and loving, but also too docile, weak, and submissive. Ant is group-minded and determined, but rarely thinks for his or herself. Buffalo is great strength and stability, but also about prosperity and blessings. Badger is aggressive and determined, which can come off as abrasive if out of balance. Crow is all about change, seeing a higher perspective, and shape-shifting, which if too extreme can come off as unstable and flighty. Butterfly is grace in action and transformative in nature, but may at times not be grounded enough for reality. Bull is fertile, raw, and charging toward things with confidence and courage, but too much Bull is stubborn, obstinate, and irritating to others.

It's all about finding the good and the bad, and coming to a harmonic balance between the two.

Through visualization and meditation we can get in touch with the spirit animals, or power animals as they are often called, that are directing our behaviors and actions, and work with them to achieve greater understanding and well-being. If one of our archetypal animal guides is too powerful (say Bear, who is powerful, instinctive, and has vast will power, but can be overwhelming and opinionated to the extreme), we may want to go into our sacred space and welcome it to come and spend time with us. Either we work with Bear to reduce the traits that we feel are out of balance, or we invite another spirit animal into our space to balance Bear, perhaps the gentle wisdom and nurturing of Deer.

Each Native tradition has its own special animals that hold archetypal meaning for those who embrace them as their spirit guides or totems. Just as in traditional astrology, these archetypes work best when their positive qualities outweigh their negative qualities, or when one archetypal animal balances another that is of an opposite nature.

Shamanic traditions have long used chanting and drumming as a means for accessing other realities where power animals and spirit guides exist. The idea was to access these guides and work with them on behalf of a sick villager or someone experiencing a problem. By using a variety of techniques to bring about an altered state of consciousness, such as chanting, music, meditation, or using a mantra, we ourselves can meet and communicate with these archetypes deep within and create the balances of power we need to experience an internal and external state of well-being.

The most important aspect of working with archetypes based on guides, whether animal, spirit, or otherwise, is to ask clear questions of them when communicating and to take note of the information received, which may be in the form of images, sounds, symbols, or direct answers. Often, the answers given are not understood right away on a conscious level and are meant to direct the subconscious mind toward a particular change or outcome, so it's important to be open, receptive, and non-analytical, especially if it doesn't make immediate sense.

Just as with all symbols, the outward appearance of an archetypal animal guide may be less about the actual traits of that animal and more about what it might represent. An example is looking at the "animal medicine" offered by each archetype. A Hawk may symbolize a need for clearer, sharper vision and a higher perspective of a situation we might be struggling with. Thus, the Hawk gives us the medicine of sharper vision, which may be more important to us than being more "hawkish" in our actions and behaviors. This is why it is important to ask questions, use intuition, and allow the subconscious to absorb the information without the blocks presented by the analytical conscious mind.

Seeing or meeting a Wolf may not be so much about the usual characteristics we think of when we see a wolf, such as courage and strength, but about focusing on the "wolf medicine" of moving confidently in our environment and feeling more comfortable in our own skin. The animal's medicine is that which balances an extreme or fills a void within that keeps us in "dis-ease."

Granted, astrology digs far deeper than just sun and moon signs and the Zodiac we know and see posted daily. There are nodes, rising signs, aspects, eclipses, and houses—all of which are said to play a role in who we are and what we will become, based upon our birth time and place and the position of stars, planets, the sun, and moon in the sky. But the solidification of each symbol is something we all express when we associate a behavior with our personal sign. Even if we consciously laugh off astrology, on the deeper levels of the mind, we buy into the symbols because they have become a part of our culture and tradition.

Relationship Archetypes of Astrology

Even in our love relationships, archetypes are working their magic or their curses. The people we attract and become involved with are not by accident, for we are expressing patterns and behaviors that are rooted in old programs and beliefs. Our relationship history is the perfect breeding ground for understanding which archetypes are messing with our abilities to find and express real love. Thus, we keep repeating painful experiences with different faces, but the characteristics are the same.

Until we look at the patterns and the archetypes beneath those patterns, we will continue to draw the same thing, including abusive, narcissistic, and emotionally unavailable partners who are trying to awaken in us the very archetypes needed to finally heal the wounded inner self. In the Vedic astrology of Hinduism, it is believed that there is an animal associated with our Moon sign and this animal governs the primal parts of our personality. There are 27 of these signs and we can gain deep psychological insight into ourselves and those we know, especially in close relationships, by understanding the interplay between signs. Once we take off the masks we show others, this animal steps up to the forefront and its qualities become apparent in our lives.

Carol Allen is a professional Vedic astrologer, relationship coach, and author of *The Five Astrological Archetypes of Relationships*. She says there are five basic archetypes that define us romantically and either enhance or hinder our chances at successful relationships: "You see, your archetype has everything to do with how you interact with and respond to others, see relationships, and experience dating and mating in general." When we become aware of them, we can then understand what we need to do to clean out old patterns and beliefs and find new ways of better relating to the opposite sex for better results.

Allen points out that as we go through life, we experience different astrological phases that will activate different aspects, or archetypes, and that they can be positively or negatively influencing our relationship to others.

The five basic archetypes she works with are:

1. The Lady in the Tower: Someone who loves to be alone, but wants a relationship. Past hurts may stop her (or him if he is a Lord!) from getting out into the world, thus going into the tower in the first place.

2. The Career Woman or Man: Focused on career and getting that degree or building a business, often to the detriment of a personal life. These types crave security and work hard to not be dependent on others, often to an extreme!

3. The Masculine Woman: With a lot of inherent masculine qualities, this archetype is an "alpha dog" who doesn't need someone else, even if she wants someone else.

4. The Highly Sensitive Woman: Everything is taken too seriously, indicating a thin skin and inability to not take things personally.

5. The Woman Who Believes Love Is Hard: Pretty self-explanatory, no? If you believe something is hard, you will experience it as such.

These are basic descriptions and anyone can get the more detailed work Allen does that is formulated to birth times and dates. Of course, these five archetypes apply to men, too, who struggle with their own blocks, patterns, and issues that keep them stuck, unhappy, and alone. The great thing is that once we identify our love type, we can begin to dissect and change it to work more in our favor by cleaning out old beliefs and perceptions that may have belonged to our parents, teachers, society, and peers. Then we can reprogram what we believe is right for us onto a clean slate.[2]

How we love, who we love, and how much love we have in our lives are all indicators of how active our archetypes are. If we are always being emotionally abused, it's time to turn off the "victim" and become more of a "goddess." If women always use us for money, we may need to power up our "warrior" and power down our "father" aspect. Perhaps we keep attaching ourselves to unavailable partners who break our hearts. Out with the "martyr" and in with the "lover" who is by nature more aware and astute at the art of all things involving the heart. Or maybe add a dash of "king" or "queen" to bolster up a poor sense of self-esteem that might be allowing repeated bad behaviors from others.

And kick all those "betrayers" to the curb!

Dreamworking

Most of us dream at night. To both Freud and Jung, the dream world was critical to understanding the inner realms of the psyche. In dreams, the conscious, literal, analytical, judgmental, and critical mind shuts down in favor of the intuitive, imaginative, subconscious, symbolic, metaphorical, and collective unconscious where the language is spoken in images and is not meant to be understood by the waking mind.

Some of our dreams may be rote and boring, or easily understood as a way of working out a problem or issue plaguing us during the day. But other dreams are chock-full of bizarre and unexplainable beings, situations, and even places that we know in our gut are "not of this world." Many suffer from night terrors and nightmares that are totally removed from our day-to-day reality, and many others have recurring dreams that seem to be trying to tell us something important, thus their recurring nature.

Dreams are the stories the mind needs to tell us that we might not pay attention to during the waking state.

Sometimes we can remember almost every detail about a dream, especially those of a terrifying nature. Other times we have no recall at all. This is because the dreams don't need to be recalled or remembered in order to affect the levels of the mind that understand what they are conveying. The conscious mind does not benefit much from "getting" a dream, because most of the programming the dream imagery needs to influence is on the subconscious and collective unconscious levels, especially as dreams seem ripe with archetypal images.

In order to work with dreams, it is incredibly helpful to notice repeated themes, images, and patterns, so it behooves us to try to recall as much as we can, especially if we feel on an intuitive level that a dream is trying to send a message. Often, this is as easy as leaving a notebook and pen beside our bed, on a table with a light, so that upon awakening we can quickly jot down what we dreamed about. For others, a small tape recorder or even the recorder on our cell phone suffices, especially if we are more expressive verbally than in writing.

Once we have begun to do this, it becomes more of a habit and we actually find our minds responding and remembering more of what we dreamt. Even if we cannot recall every single detail, strong images that shook us should be noted, as well as feelings and sensations we got while dreaming.

When it comes to interpreting our dream symbols, it can be quite a sticky issue. There are tons of books and encyclopedias about what this dream or that dream means, and sometimes those suggestions are right on the mark. But because we are all individuals, with different archetypes active, we may need to employ our own gut instinct, intuition, and discernment to understand what our own dreams mean. The images are personal to us, even if they are also universal, but for the sake of the work we are doing, we are more concerned with how these universal images and situations affect us alone.

Once we get an idea of what symbols are more often present in our dreams than others and what situations keep coming up night after night, we can begin to dissect what our deepest fears and concerns are, and which archetypes represent them. If we continuously dream of being chased by an attacker, we need to look at our lives and see where we feel we are being "attacked" by others or put in dangerous or impossible situations. Our "victim" and "innocent" have been triggered for a reason. Are we being sabotaged at work? Is a family member "out to get us"? Is a love relationship starting to feel more like we are being stalked and controlled?

Recurring dream symbols and situations tell us the most about where we are at now in our evolution and growth. This author has many dreams about being trapped by a dangerous cult, and having to desperately find a way to escape before it's too late. This can mean that the "artist" or "creator" feels suppressed by "dictators" and "rulers," or it can mean that the author feels trapped by circumstances that must be "escaped" in order to find authentic expression and happiness.

A recurring dream of a crashing plane is a popular motif of loss of control. The plane crashing indicates a sense of not having control anymore of one's own life, and that they are about to "crash and burn" if they don't find a way to get control again of the plane as it goes down. This type of dream is common during major life transitions such as moving, marriage or divorce, having a baby, or illness.

Patterns in dreams, just as patterns in normal waking behavior, come from the programming deep in the levels of the mind we must access. Patterns are giant waving red flags that indicate areas of our lives that we must work hard on if we want to move forward with clarity, focus, and purpose.

A pattern of dreaming about the death of a loved one can indicate our fear of being alone and abandoned. The "child" has been triggered, perhaps by a loss in the past (even of a pet or a favorite toy), and now the fear of someone we love passing on haunts us. Unless we processed our feelings in the past, we won't react or respond any differently to them in the present. Somehow, the "child" must be acknowledged and healed before we stop having those dreams.

In addition to the images and situations of our dreams trying to help us work through old issues and face our archetypes, dreams can also warn us about illnesses and dangers to come. Many people have precognitive dreams in which they see themselves on the surgery table or in a devastating car crash. Sometimes these dreams end up happening in the literal sense, which means there is a part of the dreaming mind that can tap into the future or see a nonlinear timeline. We might even dream of a loved one getting into trouble to find out it actually transpired, suggesting a telepathic quality to some dreams. An article titled "Can Our Dreams Solve Problems While We Sleep?" from the April 15, 2014, edition of *Psychology Today* documents intriguing research done by Carlyle Smith, a scientist working with the Department of Psychology at Canada's Trent University. Smith presented a paper on his studies involving young adults who were able to dream about the life problems of people they did not know or never met, and based simply upon seeing a photo of the other person. The studies involved 66 students who showed that they could actually dream about the "target individual" and get correct information about that person's life and problems. Many of the dream elements the students reported were quite literal, as in dreaming about specifics associated with the target in much higher proportion than normal.[3]

This mirrors dreams people have of an area on their body that suddenly begins speaking to them or an entity appears that warns them about a part of the body they must address, only to find that, upon a doctor's visit, there is cancer present. Our bodies also seem to be speaking to us in dreams, using imagery we understand both in a literal and metaphorical sense.

Carl Jung worked with dreams and believed that the way a dream ended could not be changed. He believed this because, to him, the ending was all about the subconscious mind finally getting to express the truth to the dreamer without influence of the dreamer's conscious mind. This is critical to helping the psyche understand the dream itself.

What about lucid dreaming, the ability to become aware within a dream and actually govern and change the dream itself? Is this sabotaging the efforts of the subconscious and even the unconscious and its archetypes to do the necessary work that dreams are meant to do in the first place? It very well could be best to leave our dreams alone, but many people have found relief from horrible recurring nightmares by actually "going lucid" and taking control of the outcome.

Nightmares cause us great trauma. They shake us to the core. But they are a necessary evil. According to the *Dream Interpretation Dictionary*, "Nightmares are the most misunderstood of all dreams. They are often dismissed as nothing more than the distressed images of an overactive mind." However, they serve an important purpose as a "healthy expression of deep-seated tension and fears." We need nightmares to help us vicariously deal with the "monsters" of our minds![4]

Nightmares are major stomping grounds for archetypal creatures and beasts, even human ones, that chase us, try to kill us, harm us or loved ones, and generally cause us to wake up in a cold sweat.

But the monster archetypes are helping us cope with fears we cannot deal with during the waking state, either because we would be crippled with fear and unable to function, or because they affect a deeper part of the mind the conscious cannot even comprehend.

If you tell a friend that you dreamed a big ugly ogre tried to chase you and stomp you out of existence, that friend might suggest it represents your fears and insecurities out in the world of being "stomped on" by the competition. Or maybe, to them, it signifies your constantly running from the ugliness of your marriage or job situation. Yet that big ugly ogre is an archetype for the inner monster that drives you from a foundation of fear. It's one that you need to understand and deal with so that your actions won't be based upon fear any longer, but upon authenticity and self-love. So the ogre within can be quite different than the interpretations of others, and only you know what it means.

One thing to remember is that we usually always wake up right before a monster is about to stomp on us, kill us, drown us, imprison us, torture us, and so on. We wake up before the point of death, because the dream is not about dying or even being afraid of death itself. It's about our monster archetypes asking to be heard and seen and telling us we need to confront our fears, demons, and old, negative patterns so we can be happier and more fulfilled.

By changing a nightmare into a positive lesson, we can grasp what it is trying to tell us, let the archetypes in question have their say, and then move on. Chances are, once we do this, we will no longer have that particular dream anymore.

So the three steps of working with nightmares are:

1. Recognize and acknowledge the elements of the nightmare.

2. Identify what really terrifies you about those elements and what they represent.

3. Change the negative elements into a positive lesson and conclusion, including the monster archetypes. They really are *guides* in disguise!

Lucid Dreaming

Why are some dreams fixed in stone and yet, in others, we become aware we are dreaming and can actually affect the outcome and control where we go and what happens to us? Because Jung believed that the subconscious must play a dream out to the end in order for it to really help us, what do we do with lucid dreams? Maybe they are another opportunity for us to work with the themes, motifs, and archetypes where we actually can interact with them and take back some of the negative powers we have given them.

Lucid dreaming comes easy to many, whereas others find it impossible to do voluntarily. It can be practiced to the point of becoming easier, but it's a lot of hard work. The power of going lucid in a dream could be incredibly useful, though, as a way for us to spend some time in the dream world, being with our archetypes, and even asking them questions to glean insight. Because we feel safe knowing we have control, we can engage in "fact finding missions" into our own subconscious and collective unconscious on a quest for wisdom and insight, and come back to the waking state any time we are ready.

If we go lucid in a dream unexpectedly, it offers us the chance to take back the hero archetype we may have given away to others who are always saving us. We can reclaim our inner god or goddess and become more powerful as we overcome nightmarish scenarios and face our inner demons and monsters. Lucidity is a bridge between the conscious and the deeper levels of the mind, so the work we do in a lucid state affects all three profoundly.

How can we become more adept at lucid dreaming? Some of the tips we can practice include:

1. Keep our dream journal on a bedside table where we can easily reach it upon waking.

2. Make sure we are comfortable and, when fully relaxed, tell ourselves we intend to lucid dream.

3. Repeat this intention until we are asleep, embedding into the dreaming levels of the mind to improve our odds of going lucid. You can say out loud something such as "I am aware that I am lucid dreaming" or "I am aware I am dreaming."

4. Upon waking, record the dream memories and whether or not we were lucid part of the time, the whole time, or not at all. Your personal dream journal will show you recurring signs, symbols, and situations that play a large role in your dreaming and waking state.

5. If desired, use guided meditations and visualizations specifically designed to encourage lucid dreaming.[5]

Though we will not be completely "awake" in the dream, it will feel as though we are, and we can even intend before we fall asleep that we will ask a certain question, or guide the dream in a certain direction and location. The more we practice, the more we will notice becoming lucid and taking advantage of the opportunities to do a little sleuthing in the parts of our minds we don't normally have access to. We may also notice that when we awaken from a lucid dream, say to use the bathroom or get a drink of water, we often go back to sleep and pick right up where the dream left off! Again, this may be the subconscious mind demanding we get all the way to the ending so it can get what it needs from the dream experience.

Do our dreams mirror life, or does our life mirror dreams? It's probably a bit of both because as we work with dream images, archetypes, and motifs, we find our waking life changing for the better. Also, as we make changes to our lives on the conscious level, we often find our dreams shifting to reflect those changes, or to awaken and alert us to new issues we need to address. If we are going to spend a great deal of time in the dream state, then we might as well make it work for our benefit.

Spending time romping around with our archetypes is a necessity to allow them full expression, which we usually deny them during the waking state. This is especially true of the archetypes we consider more taboo or undesirable. They need to be heard and seen, or they will cause us more grief in the form of recurring night-mares and disturbing dreams that leave us feeling like zombies upon awakening. Dreams are the opportunities for our archetypes to tell us their stories of how they came to be, what they want, and how we can use them for our benefit or detriment, depending on whether or not we acknowledge them. They also allow us to live with fears that would destroy us on the conscious level, processing them so that we can keep them under our control and not the other way around.

In dreams, we can let our inner archetypes have their time of expression, especially those we don't give much conscious attention to. We can also learn which of our archetypes need to simmer down and take more of a backseat in our lives, and which ones can't get a word in edgewise and are crying out for some love and attention.

Reduce, Reuse, and Recycle

Once we narrow down the archetypes we need to work with, the final step is to decide to reduce their power in our lives, reuse them as is, or recycle them for new symbols that are more empowering. Imagine having several large bins set out before us. We can throw the stuff we need to continue to work on in one bin. The stuff we can no longer use at all goes to the Archetype Recycling Plant. And the stuff we want to save because it works well goes in another bin.

By keeping them separate in our minds, we get rid of clutter and chaos, especially the unwanted archetypes we hoard and are afraid to let go of. If they no longer serve us, let them be recycled into something useful for someone else in the collective unconscious. We don't need them anymore, and by keeping them around in the closet "just in case," we are only inviting default behaviors to pop up again in our lives. Ain't nobody got time for that!

Cleaning out the clutter of the conscious, subconscious, and the unconscious levels of the mind gives us more clarity and focus so that we can move toward the life we now want to live, as the person we want to be. Just as a house full of junk makes it hard to move from room to room, a mind full of clutter makes it difficult to move from old to new.

For those archetypes we hope to reduce in power, they can stay, but put them in places where they won't interfere with the workings of the key empowering archetypes we've chosen to live by. Find a nice walk-in closet in the mind where they can hang out in comfort and not make too much of a fuss until we call them into service as needed. Often, they will rise up and protest, wanting to be acknowledged. Do so, but tell them to stay in their own space until further notice.

A clear mind is a powerful mind. But just as we wouldn't only clean one floor of a three-story home, we wouldn't declutter one level of the mind, especially when we understand how all three levels work together and often sabotage one another. This is a process that will no doubt be repeated many times. That's okay because we are always changing and evolving as we become more authentic and so, then, are the archetypes we need to reduce, reuse, and recycle. So keep those bins handy!

Life Stages

Different stages of life call for different aspects of ourselves to come into power or exit stage right. Situations such as puberty, first menstruation, first dates, marriages, divorces, baptisms, and even that old midlife crisis will activate archetypes that may have been dormant before. These life stages or situations are great times to rearrange our archetypal priorities to better reflect what we are going through.

In her goddess work, Jean Shinoda Bolen suggests women adopt certain deities during life transitions, such as Hecate, the goddess of intuitive and psychic wisdom, who can offer insight and direction when women are going through a transition. Maybe a fun-loving and sexual goddess such as Uzume, goddess of healing laughter, needs to be called into service when we are struggling with express-ing a healthy sexuality. The Hindu Kali, goddess of destruction and wrath, is a wonderful helper when we need to break down old pat-terns and destroy old ways of being.[6]

Obviously, men can call upon their inner gods or even ask their feminine aspects for help if they need balance in those areas, too.

Entering the dating world requires we activate our "lovers" and keep our "victims" in check, so that we can experience enjoyable interactions and not get used and abused. Getting a first job asks that we fire up the "leader" and "student" all in one so that we can learn and excel at what we are doing, and maybe get promoted to a higher paying position with more responsibilities. We may also need to activate the "diplomat" to get along with our colleagues, and tone down the "dictator" that might get us fired!

Marriage is a scary proposition for many, and a joyful one at the same time. It is ripe with opportunities for working with situ-ational archetypes because it forces us to grow up, become mature individuals, and act like adults. The "child" gives way to the "lover" and "friend." The "trickster" and "fool" calm down and evolve into someone responsible and a little more serious about his or her place in the world. The "prince" and "princess" evolve into "king" and "queen," as they should. Soon, "father" and "mother" may emerge as having children becomes part of the bigger picture. Marriage brings out our "god" and "goddess" during the honeymoon stage, and our "partner" and "companion" for the long haul.

Divorce is a difficult life transition for anyone. Even amicable di-vorces can take an emotional toll, and things can go a lot smoother for all parties involved if we avoid letting our "judges," "dictators," and "avengers" have too much control. Instead, we can lean on our "diplomats" and work toward a settlement that benefits both par-ties. We might also need to activate our "fathers" and "mothers" and think of the children involved, to make sure they are loved and cared for despite the breakup of the marriage.

Midlife brings even more challenges, including a full-blown crisis. This is when many men, and some women, revert back to "prince" and "princess," shunning their adult responsibilities to become a freewheeling "rebel," "stud," or "femme fatale" again. Often the results are harmful to those around us, who come up against the "betrayer" and the "cheater," or have to deal with the "child" all over again who wants a sports car when funds are tight. Women may feel like their "goddess" is no competition for the young and lovely "princesses" and "maidens" running around. The "tempters" and "temptresses" are everywhere, calling us away from the stable life we feel is stifling our creative and sexual urges.

One of the hardest life stages to deal with for either gender is old age. In our society, older people are seen as useless, invisible, and used up. Other cultures revere their elderly, even elevate them in society, but Western cultures tend to shun people who are no longer of reproducible age. This is a perfect time to call forth the "crone" and the "queen," "wise elder" and "king," and celebrate the experiences, insights, and wisdom the years have given us, instead of crying and mourning the loss of our attractiveness, sex appeal, and ability to have offspring. In our later years, we get to become "sages," "mentors," "teachers," and "visionaries" because of all we have seen, done, and been through. If we treat ourselves as worthy of these archetypes, we just might begin to change the negative connotations that growing old brings.

The more we can step into our power in any phase or stage of life, the easier and happier we will be, and we will set the stage for a better experience of those stages for our children and their children to follow. Imagine helping our children navigate things like puberty and adolescence with more grace and even excitement because we have taught them to activate positive archetypes over negative ones. We can empower them to deal with bullies at an early age by showing them how to step into their "hero" and "leader" archetypes, and leave their "victim" at home.

The final stage of life is characterized by the realization that we are mortal and that our death is coming soon. How helpful would it be to go into this time feeling more like an old sage or wise woman, rather than a useless and purposeless senior citizen? We can reframe the senior years as a powerful time to step into our experiences, wisdom, and insights to share with those who come after us, and become mentors, teachers, visionaries, and role models.

Going Within

There are so many ways to work with archetypes, and chances are one or two will suit each of us. Some therapists and life coaches encourage things such as automatic writing to allow the subconscious mind to speak while the conscious mind is quiet. Writing without censoring is a great way to see what the deeper levels of the mind have to say because the analytical critic is not operating and editing as we go along.

Tarot cards, which themselves are filled with archetypal symbols, are another way to work with aspects of our personalities, whether we do the readings ourselves or have someone adept in tarot read for us. The Major and Minor Arcanas are based upon archetypes and those who believe in synchronicity and destiny look not just at the symbols on the cards themselves, but the entire layout of the chosen cards during a reading.

There are 78 cards in a typical deck of tarot, with 22 of those as the Major Arcana, and the other 56 as the Minor Arcana. The Major Arcana are image cards that convey powerful, often intuitive responses. The imagery is transcendent and therefore understood more by the subconscious and collective unconscious where the language of symbols is loud and clear.

Again, the meanings of tarot card symbols are open to quite a bit of interpretation, but the key is finding a deck that resonates within. Some imagery may not appeal to our subconscious and unconscious, whereas other decks may offer artwork that we automatically "feel" on an intuitive level connects with our own archetypes within. There are dozens of beautiful decks now to choose from, but again, be careful of taking interpretations literally because they vary with each card reader. Instead, work with your own intuition when the chosen cards are revealed and write down what you sense they are trying to tell you about yourself.

Some therapies involve the use of music and guided imagery to work with archetypes. These are powerful tools for getting the mind into an altered state, which enhances the power and the potential to reach the deeper levels of consciousness where the important work has to be done. The goal is always individuation and the wholeness of an integrated self.

Past life recall through hypnosis is another way of accessing archetypes that may have been inherent at birth. Many people believe that their past lives continue to influence their present and future lives, and if that is true, then it makes sense that archetypes of the life we lived before might have hung on for the ride as we came into this new incarnation. Perhaps they are causing us grief and misery now because we don't want or need them, but they came with us with our DNA. Through past life clearing work, we can eliminate any negative archetypal influences and choose to keep any positive ones.

This kind of work is best done with a professional who can guide the hypnosis process and work with the client while they are under to help them identify past life situations and archetypes that are still active. All of the work we are doing here is to stop repeating the patterns of the past, and in order to make that work we have to tackle those that came from the pasts we lived before. Otherwise we will continue to see them sneakily manifest in insidious ways in the present and future.

Even something as simple as being out in nature, meditating on the beach, or sitting amongst the trees, journal in hand, can be sacred spaces for accessing our collective unconscious and allowing the archetypes to come to the surface and speak to us. Because their language is not heard in shouts and yells, we have to become aware and centered enough to discern them from our own habitual thoughts of surface mind.

People who love to express themselves artistically can draw or paint their archetypes and alter their appearances according to the new traits they want them to convey. Writers can write, poets can create poems, and dancers can use interpretive dance to express their inner transformations. It doesn't matter how we do it, as long as we find the ways that most resonate with ourselves and not just do what we were told to. So if something is not in this book, try it out!

Because archetypes are energy at their core, many choose to do energy work to balance them. Meditating on the chakras or energy centers, acupuncture, yoga, chanting, drumming, repeated movement, and other means of raising energy are tools for shifting and realigning the energy fields of the archetypes to integrate them into our own. T'ai chi, exercising, and even running allow the use of body movements to help bring the archetype energies into harmony with the physical as well as the mental. If the body is off, the mind will be, and vice versa. So when working with new or revised energies, it is incredibly helpful to include the physical body as a part of the process.

Anything that helps us relax, quiet the chatter of the surface monkey mind, and turn within will work to open the doorways to that collective unconscious level where gifts and treasures lay waiting for us to discover. But we also have as much to learn and recognize in a crowded room full of partiers, at our jobs, in our homes with our loved ones, and how we act, behave, and respond in the world at large.

Life is a playground and a school, and everything we experience is a lesson in what makes us happy, fulfilled, and purposeful, including the things that do not. Sometimes the latter speak even louder, because misery loves to shout and adores company! But we can learn from it all if we open our eyes, our minds, and our hearts to the symbolic archetypes that sit at the very center of our beings.

[chapter 8]

New Narrative, New You

So now that we've told our stories, dug up the archetypes and examined them, and determined which we needed to replace or cast out altogether, we can tell a whole new story. We've reduced the hidden symbols working in our collective unconscious minds to the ones we feel truly mirror our authentic selves. We've put back into use the ones that were always working for us, not against us. And we've given back to the universe the ones we don't want anymore, because they no longer serve the self and bring balance, harmony, and wholeness.

So where do we go from here? We write a new story. We introduce the new archetypes, character and situational, into the narrative, and weave them in with the existing archetypes from the past. We formulate a new narrative entirely, with perhaps the same destination or one that we've adjusted our sails to reach based on the new identities we've embraced. We set a new course, with our allies and guides beside us.

We are still not a tabula rasa or blank slate because, remember, we are bringing with us the past aspects of self that worked and resonated as being authentic. But we are writing a new book with new chapters, which we will fill in as we go along. And no, we are not going back to rewrite the story of the past, but instead the one that will take us into the future.

Here, we don't expect to be able to write out our new story in detail quite yet, but a great exercise for merging all that we have learned is this:

Write out a "dream vision" of your life based upon the new archetypes you are working with, as well as the old that were not recycled back to the universe, and how you imagine it might unfold were there no obstacles to your happiness, success, or achievement. What would that look like? More importantly, how would that feel? You can write three pages or 300, but put in enough detail of what you want to have and feel to get excited about actually turning it into action.

Who Are You, Revisited

Who are you now? What does this new you want? Where does this new you want to go? And what does this new you want to accomplish, for yourself and for the world? You can break it down into five-year goals if you wish, or just plot out the next year if you cannot seem to grasp that far into the future. But try.

Who am I now?

What do I want for my life now?

What do I feel is my purpose?

What is the first step I can take toward that purpose?

Where do I want to see myself in a year, five years, 10 years?

Who do I want to be in a year, five years, 10 years?

How will the new me handle what the old me couldn't?

How will my archetypes come to my aid and help me?

By asking these questions, you can get a template for your future that includes the highest and most authentic expression of self based upon all the prior work you've done. It does you no good to go back to the old story and goals. You are a new *you* now. You are *more you* now.

Sometimes a whole new story is needed to overcome past challenges. But usually we can hold onto the past, reframe it to serve us in the present, and then let it go. After all, we cannot relive or redo what was, but we sure can live better and do better in the present and future.

Regular Check-Ups

We would never buy a car and just let it go. We would never get a diagnosis of an illness and just ignore it afterward. We would get in the habit of regular check-ups, whether for our cars or our bodies. With this work, it is no different. We can clean house and create a new narrative filled with wonderful new archetypes, go forth and be bad-ass, and take names, but at some point, we are going to have to go in for a check-up. At some point, there will be a new need to reduce, reuse, or recycle an archetypal pattern or two.

The work doesn't stop once you stop doing it once! Say that 10 times fast. So how do you know how often to dive back in and redo this work? It's pretty easy. We will know by how we feel and by how happy, fulfilled, and satisfied we are with our lives. That doesn't mean every day will be blissful and joyful, but if we are operating continuously out of an authentic place, we won't be whining, complaining, and watching aspects of ourselves and our lives fall apart.

So, when our "engine light" comes on, we take it as a warning that something needs to be revisited or addressed. We go back and redo the work in this book; we find what isn't working and replace it with what will. Because we are works in progress, we are always growing and evolving. Along with that growth comes the necessity for pruning back a few branches now and then, so we can grow even more.

We may still find we have patterns we haven't quite gotten rid of yet, and need to go back and dig the archetypes up again. Maybe we left a few in the dirt we didn't want to face on the first go-around. They will catch up with us. Or maybe new life circumstances trigger new activations of other archetypes that we were perfectly content with, but they are now out of balance and causing us grief and distress. It's time to look them in the eye and either find balance or replace them.

The road to becoming Self, whole and complete and harmonious as a mix of light and shadow, is a long one, but it doesn't have to be a continuously difficult one if we fix problems and issues and face challenges and obstacles when they first appear, rather than waiting until they've done some major damage to our psyches.

Expanding the Narrative

As we go through the rest of our lives, chances will arise to expand the narrative and bring in new situations and new characters. If we stay focused on the authentic path, the one we worked so hard to choose for ourselves and the one that truly reflects who we are, it should be easy to weed out anyone and anything we need to avoid or walk away from.

One of the benefits of readjusting our archetypes is the new knowledge we take with us into the future. Between that new level of self-awareness and the gut instinct based on the whisperings of the subconscious and the collective unconscious, we are now pay-ing attention to red flags and warning signs that could cause us to default back into old behaviors or get us into choppy waters again. If it does happen, instead of punishing ourselves, we can simply go back and do the right exercises needed to remind us of who we are and get back on track.

New experiences should not ever be feared because they are the stuff great lives are made of. But we can all too easily fall back into comfort zones, even after creating powerful new symbols to live our lives by. Habits form and we get used to things as they now are. How will we know if we are back in that comfortable place where we are just coasting by? We will feel it. The powerful, expressive, bold, and courageous archetypes within us will begin to rebel and speak out, begging for authenticity to return.

A life story doesn't end, even with death, because our legacy lives on in those who knew and loved us, and in the work we left behind. The archetypes continue even after we are gone, expressing and influencing our children and their children. Thus, it behooves us to make the symbols of our lives the best and the most inspiring they can be.

Out With the Old

The use of rituals to let go of the old parts of us can help so-lidify our new image. Sometimes we need to mark such transfor-mational times in life with a celebration or even a quiet meditative act. Whatever method we choose, it is important to literally and symbolically say goodbye to the old us and welcome in the new.

One way to do this is to take an old photo of a time in our lives that most represented the challenges and issues we want to say goodbye to, or we can go back to the origin point of the worst of the archetypes we have chosen to rid ourselves of. Taking the photo, we can go to a sacred place in nature, the ocean, or even our own backyard, and light the picture on fire, saying a prayer silently or out loud to burn away the old habits, thoughts, and behaviors and cleanse us for the new.

Perhaps name the archetypes being "burned away," but do so with love, not anger or hatred. Remember, these were aspects of the self that once helped us survive or that we didn't consciously choose. We did the best we could at the time, so gently let the ashes fly off into the wind.

Then take a photograph of the new "you" and keep it as a reminder of who you are now.

Another ritual involves the use of candles and the symbolism of light and dark. Buy two candles, one dark and one white. Light the dark candle first. Over the dark candle, list the parts of you that no longer serve you, then say goodbye and blow out the candle. Now light the white candle while listing the powerful new symbols you have chosen that best represent the real you. Let the white candle burn awhile as you go about your day, reminding you to stay true to the new you.

Any kind of ritual will work that involves the two parts—saying goodbye and saying hello—so use your imagination. There is incredible power to rituals, as they are meant to be understood on a subconscious level as well as the unconscious, where symbols speak louder than they do in the conscious mind. The work itself was analytical, left-brained, and conscious at times, so this is a wonderful opportunity to seal the deal on all levels of the mind and integrate the new behaviors and characteristics fully.

For many, journaling can be a great way to complete the journey taken. Though a lot of writing has already been required, some find that jotting down thoughts about what has transpired is a way to "fix" their new reality into place. But anything works. Write a song or a poem. Do an interpretive dance or create art that expresses the emergence of the authentic person you have become. Draw images of the new archetypes and give them fun names!

Our ancestors knew the profound power of ritual and it has been a part of who we are as human beings as we have evolved. It can be an amazing tool for feeling a sense of completion and accomplishment, and marking the progress and transformations we have made in a way that makes them more memorable and symbolic.

Celebrate with a party or go out alone! Read a good book. Take a mini-vacation. Make an ice cream sundae. Treat and reward yourself for a job well done. It doesn't matter, as long as it feels good and gives a nice send-off to the old and a warm and exciting welcome to the new.

Speak the Truth

We've all heard about the Law of Attraction (LOA) teachings that state what you focus on expands and what you give attention to is what you see more of in your life. Many people attest to the power of the LOA in their own lives, and it makes incredible sense that the words and beliefs that we express the most reflect what we will draw to us in new experiences, simply because we don't have the capacity yet for new beliefs and experiences that draw to us anything better.

In her book *Warrior Goddess Training: Becoming the Woman You Are Meant to Be*, Heatherash Amara writes, "Transformation starts with how we use our words—how we speak our story to ourselves and others. Like body and mind, words are vessels. Each word we choose can hold the vibration of healing, peace, and love, or be brimming with victimization and judgment." The things we tell ourselves matter because they express our deepest beliefs and, often, we aren't even aware of these tapes playing in a loop in our minds.[1]

In the 12-step recovery movement, there is some controversy as to whether or not it is helpful to have alcoholics, addicts, and codependents get up in front of a room full of people and say "Hi, I'm ------, and I'm an alcoholic/addict/codependent" because continuously identifying with the disease perpetuates it. The Law of Attraction would say this is true and that anytime we convince ourselves that we are this or that, we cannot change. Perhaps a better way is to say the word "recovering" or even "recovered" and begin to identify with someone who is no longer what is trying to be avoided.

This is not to say that the 12-step movement is wrong, because alcoholism and addiction doesn't go away that easily and the idea is a person is only one drink or drugging away from going back into full-blown addiction. But there is something to be said for empowering the words we use to describe who we are and who we hope to be.

Now that we have become this new identity with new behaviors, attitudes, and beliefs about ourselves, we must watch what we say so that we don't go back into old default habits. This is especially critical when we backslide, which we will—often! Instead of telling ourselves what failures we are because we slipped back into an old pattern, we must continue to strive toward the vision of what we want to be, and our language and thoughts must be gently prodded back into alignment with that vision.

As Heatherash Amara writes in *Warrior Goddess Training*, we must not just find our authentic voice, but maintain it. "When you deny your own voice, this feeds your judge or victim voices, rather than your authenticity, and the result is anger at yourself and others."[2] Thus, we fall back into those default archetypes of "victim," "judge," and even "abused," and everything else we just worked so hard to transform.

Remember, the ultimate goal of this work is to create wholeness between the self and shadow self and bring harmony and balance into our lives. Doing so means empowering the aspects that bring us more of what we want and disempowering those that bring us more of what we don't want. Caroline Myss writes in *Sacred Contracts: Awakening Your Divine Potential* that "Your highest potential, then, is the part of you that is not limited to its expression by the fears of the physical world and the business of living. It is what you actualize when you are willing to confront your shadow, openly acknowledge the reality of its presence within you, and then take steps to deal with it."

Myss goes on to say that examining the shadow allows us to see who we would be if we were expressing our highest potential, and living with the knowledge that genuine power comes from inside of us, not external things. This leads to authentic living and allows us to be our real selves in the world, and to lead by example in helping others find their own authentic selves, too.[3]

But it all really does start with the thoughts we allow to run through our minds unchecked. Thoughts are made up of words we don't speak out loud, so we must remain vigilant to both what we think and what we say, and make sure it is aligned with our vision, not someone else's or society's vision for us.

One of this author's favorite exercises is "Cancel, Cancel." It's pretty simple, but effective. Every time you find yourself saying something negative or acting or reacting from old habits and default modes, you stop and say, "Cancel, Cancel" and then immediately correct the thoughts, actions, and behaviors to your new default. Canceling out the old negative thoughts is a great way to become aware of how often you talk down to yourself and how often you let your negative archetypes have their say. Shut them and yourself up and reframe those words with positive, present-based affirmations that empower and strengthen, not disempower and weaken.

Eventually, the subconscious catches up to the new vision and programming it is receiving on a regular basis because, remember, that old programming was deeply entrenched. So we have to repeat things continuously, like a broken record, for the subconscious to finally accept it as the new reality. The more feeling we put behind the new affirmative statements, the quicker the subconscious finds a place for them to be firmly entrenched as our new reality, so feel what you say and think!

Then, the same thing occurs on the level of the collective un-conscious. Even though at this level we are exposed to the influ-ences of universal energies and archetypes of others and the world around us, we are much more empowered to choose which we acknowledge as our own and which we want active in our immediate, personal world.

It has been suggested that it takes approximately 21 to 28 days to ingrain a new habit in our minds, so it might take awhile before we begin to realize we are talking and thinking more powerful words, and even acting on them. We will backslide, and that's fine, as long as we bring ourselves back into alignment by focusing on what we want and not what we want to stop doing. (Remember, you can never get enough of what you don't want, right?)

Parent the Lost Child

No doubt much of what we uncover through this work goes back to situations and events from our childhood, when we were left abandoned, alone, scared, unsure, lost, and helpless. Whether our childhood was somewhat idyllic or filled with abuse and neglect, we all suffer as children by the sheer fact that, at the time, we are being exposed to the ways of a world that is not always kind, loving, caring, or compassionate. That is a part of growing up.

Often as adults, we have forgotten that wounded and lost child we once were. We mistakenly think we can navigate adulthood without ever having to acknowledge that child again. But we are wrong. The "child" archetype must be dealt with in order for us to become fully authentic and whole.

Any of the tools in this book can be used to heal that child within, but guided meditation is one of the best this author has encountered for actually going into a sacred mental space, asking the child to come forward, and then asking he or she what is needed to integrate the child into who we see ourselves as becoming. Do we want to carry around a wounded, lost, and frightened child? No, but what we can do in the process of visualization is ask our inner child what he or she needs to feel loved, cared for, heard, seen, and acknowledged. This is the process of re-parenting, for whether we had great parents or awful parents, as children we often felt invisible and unloved, no matter the circumstances.

If our childhoods include forms of sexual, physical, and emotional abuse or mental illness, it is critical to do this work. A good idea is to work with a professional to assure that we can handle the triggering of events and situations that caused trauma. Children do suffer from PTSD (post-traumatic stress disorder), just as soldiers, rape victims, and victims of violent crimes do, and this author can attest to that, having a child who was treated for PTSD after a series of traumatic surgeries in his early childhood. That PTSD doesn't always dissipate and can still be driving certain thoughts and behaviors in us even today.

So while we are revisiting and cleaning out the archetypes that no longer work in our favor or align with the truth of who we are, we must do the re-parenting of the "child" so that we can embrace that archetype and its innocence, goodness, and awe without also taking on its fears, hopelessness, and weaknesses. We must become the "father" or "mother" to that "child" we did not have in the past, or we had, but in a dysfunctional enough manner to cause us harm.

There are many books and workshops about healing the wounded inner child, and we can do simple guided meditations at home that allow us to literally meet ourselves at particular ages, when situations defined us in ways that no longer benefit us. We can sit in our sacred space and talk to the inner child, the inner adolescent, the inner teen, and young adult and find out exactly what they require for healing. This work takes time and is not to be rushed because that baggage being carried by the child within didn't accumulate overnight. In some cases, it's been with us for decades.

Start with a guided meditation that takes you to your favorite sacred place within. First, call up your young child, the youngest you can, and sit with that child for awhile. Talk to him or her. Find out what hurts and why. Take him or her into your arms and let the tears flow. Then ask how you can heal the deep wounds. Listen for instructions and insights. Promise your inner child you will be his or her "warrior" and "parent," and embrace them into yourself. Once you truly feel they are a part of you now as an adult and that they are comfortable and safe, come out of your sacred space. During the next few weeks and months, that small child may ask to be heard again and again. Listen. Just doing the visualization is not enough if they still have something to say. If we continue to not listen to them, they get louder and louder, usually in the form of attracting what we don't want to experience, or manifesting in bad behaviors that will get us into trouble.

Repeat this process with any age necessary to bring about a strong sense of integration. This is a similar process to the one used by psychologists to integrate personalities in people suffering from dissociative identity disorder. Think about it. In a way we all suffer from multiple personalities, and they manifest as the archetypes that are asking to be heard and acknowledged. Our main conscious personality may or may not be aware of the other "alters," but they are there, influencing and affecting the main personality in all kinds of hidden ways. The "child" is one of the most vocal because we all have a childhood we need to revisit and reframe if we are to really move forward as adults.

No matter how we choose to work with the inner "child," it has to happen before we can feel complete. A lost "child" is manifested as a broken aspect of the adult and will continue to create negative and painful patterns of behavior if not addressed, worked with, and eventually healed and integrated into the adult.

Change the External

Perhaps all that inner change has made us feel restless and caused us to desire some changes in our external world. This is one of the most enjoyable aspects of inner transformation—getting to change things up a little (or a lot) in our immediate environment. Those positive changes we make within need to find a mirror without, or we will walk around feeling incongruous, inharmonious, and unauthentic.

So we can start by looking at our new archetypes and our new identity and find ways to bring that same authenticity to our homes and special spaces, including how we look, dress, act, speak, and carry ourselves. Even the cars we drive and the clothes we wear may change, as well as the food we eat and the way we move our bodies.

From the standpoint of who we now wish to be, are we carrying that into how we present ourselves to the world? Say we have gone from "victim" to "goddess" (or "god"). How might we still be playing small with our own appearance, bodies, or the clothes we wear? What would a "goddess" look like? No, we don't have to have the perfect body and figure, but we can certainly start dressing in a way a true "goddess" would and carrying ourselves taller and with purpose.

From the time we are very young, we have preferences. Some may prefer to be out in the dirt and mud in jeans and a T-shirt, others like the look of a pretty, feminine dress or a masculine suit. With time, we start to dress for comfort and to please others, or in many cases, to hide our true selves from the world for fear of becoming a "victim" or being put in the spotlight of attention. This is especially true of many women who were sexually abused as children, who later go on to hide their bodies in clothing that is way too big and unattractive because they don't want the attention of the opposite sex. A young boy might begin wearing only suits as a teenager to appease his father, who insists he put on a professional front. But maybe that young boy wants to wear jeans and a black leather jacket that is more fitting to his suppressed inner "rebel."

There are so many reasons why we don't make ourselves look and feel our best, or at least the way we want to look and feel, were the considerations and judgments of others not a factor.

But now is the time to dress as we want and express our authenticity. Flowing gowns? Why not? Elvis's blue suede shoes? Go for it! Wear makeup, cut your hair short, dye it purple, and do whatever makes you feel like the real *you* that has been buried under archetypes that never let it breathe.

You don't like the home you are living in because it doesn't reflect you? Change it. You don't have to necessarily sell the house, but if you can afford to, move into a home that truly resonates with you and feels like a "home," not just a house. If you stay where you are, what is stopping you from a complete re-do? Renovate, redesign, and reflect who you are now in the rooms you call your home. You have to spend most of your time there, so why not remake it to align with the new identity you have taken on?

Do you hate the car you drive? Think about trading it in, or if you still like the car but it's in need of work, get it fixed up and painted. Find a way to trade it in for something that you can see yourself driving. If you can't afford to do that right now, then love the car you are with until you can, always keeping your eyes on the prize. That mini-van that served its purpose when your kids were small is not making you happy anymore. Brainstorm ways to buy or lease the little compact car you long to drive that better suits your sporty spirit.

How about your job? Do you hate it? Does it steal your spirit having to go to a job that drains you of energy? Find a way to either make the job you have more suited to who you are, or change jobs. If you have the entrepreneur archetype in your veins, start working on ways to start your own business doing something you actually want to do, something you love and feel passionate about! We spend so much of our lives at our jobs; shouldn't they at least reflect aspects of who we are that we like and enjoy?

Is your relationship making you sick? Are you spending time with toxic people too often? Do you have family members that are so dysfunctional they make your head spin? One of the hardest, but most emotionally and spiritually rewarding things you can do is to review the people you spend the most time with and decide whether they are worthy of your time, love, and energy.

Take a good hard look at lovers, friends, and colleagues, as well as family, and determine who is draining and negative. Who sabotages and undermines you? Who judges and condemns your goals and dreams? Those people have got to go if you ever hope to live an authentic life expressing who you are. Maybe in the past they served a purpose, to remind you of the parts of yourself that you most needed to change and work on, but now that you have, keeping them in your life will not serve the new growth you've experienced and hope to continue experiencing.

You don't have to be unkind, but you do have to be kind first and foremost to yourself. If a relationship of any kind has run its course and is now causing harm to you and the other person, it's time to either renegotiate the terms or end the contract outright. Remember, you can change a situation, accept a situation, or walk away from a situation. The same goes for relationships.

Look, this is your life! Nobody is stopping you from having the things that feel right but you. Your past beliefs about yourself and your life kept you believing that what you had was what you really wanted, but you know better. It's time to ask, "What do I want for me now?"

Love gardens? Go plant one. Enjoy the sound of animals playing in the yard? Adopt a couple of shelter dog pals. Enjoy flowers, but have no one to give them to you? Go to the market and buy fresh flowers to adorn your home or plant some where you can outside. Have a condo? Put some planters on the balcony or patio.

All of the work you have done inside is well and good, but if you are still trapped in a dingy environment surrounded by things you don't want, people you can't stand, and stuff you don't need, then change it to show the new you. Reclaim your life. Visualize what you want it to be like. Journal, meditate, and speak words that attract this truth and not the old.

Envisioning the Future

One of the most important archetypes we can embrace is our inner "visionary," because once we do the work of transformation and growth, we do need to envision our new life, especially our future and the way we now wish it to unfold. Though we cannot predict everything we will encounter, we can, in guided meditation or visualization, begin to see the life we hope to manifest.

Part of envisioning the future involves more than just seeing what we want for ourselves and our own lives. It also means coming to understand how our lives reflect upon and influence the lives of others. Where before we may have caused much harm to others, now we can be a light to them. Where in the past we might have treated people with disregard, so caught up in our own dreams, now we can see them for who they really are and help them be the best they can be by our example.

This is the time we call into play the archetypes most responsible for reaching new heights of expression, fulfillment, happiness, and success. We bring in our "leader" and "mentor" more often. We look to our "sage" and our "wizard" to help us navigate this brave, new world. We act like the "kings and queens" that we are, and try to be our own "heroes," as well as "heroes" to those who ask for our help. We are "teachers" now, sharing what we've learned with others so they, too, can transform their lives. We are "lovers" in the best sense of the word, and "warriors" for justice, peace, and equality.

Will we be remembered as a loving "warrior" for justice, or go back to being a "victim"? Will those who come after us say we were a kindhearted "queen" or a compassionate "king"? Will we be a "guide" to those who needed direction and a "mentor" to the young? A joyful "sidekick" who was always there for his or her friends? We have the power to become the "leaders," "creators," and "visionaries" we always imagined we could be now.

The stories that tell the world who we are and what we are made of are ours alone to write, and now we have the tools to write the best stories we possibly can envision for ourselves. We also have the new understanding that change happens on more than just the topsoil of the mind. It has to also occur deep where the roots of our beliefs, attitudes, and identities take root.

Personally, we want to be happy and live a life of purpose, right? We don't necessarily have to be rich, famous, or perfect, although if those things hold appeal, go for it. There is nothing wrong with wanting to be rich, famous, or beautiful. There is nothing wrong with wanting anything, unless that want becomes an obsession that hurts us and others. But we do want to enjoy the time we have been given on this dimension and experience more love than hate, more kindness than violence, and more light than darkness. Our chosen archetypes are tools and a means to that end, but they are also a part of the most foundational aspect of who we are. They have served us well, even the ones that we had to get rid of or change, because at the time when we embraced them and related to them, we needed what they had to teach us.

But now is a new day. We have the power to change so many things about ourselves and the environment we live in, from our appearances to jobs to who we love, laugh, and live with. We can be just about anything we want in terms of vocation. We can express ourselves in ways we never imagined before thanks to advances in technology that allow us to reach out to people all over the world in a matter of minutes.

Without a strong vision for ourselves, we tend to fall back into accepting the visions of others around us who think they know what is best for us. We need our own brass ring to reach for and our own goals, dreams, and aspirations. Others can suggest and be helpful, but they cannot create for us the life we alone desire. That's our job.

For the Global Good

Collectively, the same is true. Whether we are talking about our family of origin, our neighborhood, our nation, or our planet, we can change things. But to do so, we must stop the wheel from turning every now and then, and take time to really examine the foundation of our existence for cracks and holes. If we fail to do this, the damage done could be permanent.

How often does society as a whole get the opportunity to really dig deep and identify the driving forces and factors behind global consciousness and behavior? Probably not enough. In fact, it often takes a major disaster or tragedy of epic proportions to wake up the collective and make us question who we are, how we are behaving, and whether or not we need to change.

Using the tools in this book and many others, we can try to avoid hitting a personal or collective bottom before we make what is not working either work correctly, or replace it with what does. One only needs to turn on the morning news to see that many of the global symbols and archetypes we live by are harmful to us, others, and the environment. Can we afford to continue to ignore them and not change our story, not replace those archetypes with ones that better serve humanity and the living things we share the planet with?

Personal awakening and transformation happens when we have the courage as individuals to say "Enough of this," identify exactly what "this" is, and then do the hard, often brutal work of changing it to "that." Not everyone feels the need to break out of his or her comfort zone to make that hero's journey, but for those who do, the treasure of a new and better life is the reward. In turn, others live by the example of those brave enough to leap into a new life. Like a ripple from a stone tossed into the pond, the awakening spreads. It goes viral.

Only when we get to that tipping point where enough people are making this journey and changing the archetypes that are stale, ineffective, and even dangerous, will the collective begin to lean more to the side of all things good. That is not to say there will be no more villains and outlaws, victims and abusers, devils, manipulators, and charmers. The shadow will always be around because without it, the self is not whole and complete.

But there will be more heroes, gods, goddesses, warriors, mothers, fathers, protectors, visionaries, mentors, and a whole lot more to keep the scales erring on the side of the light. Imagine the power of creators and activists working together to solve the world's problems. The pendulum always swings back and forth, but imagine a world where it doesn't swing to such extremes because a majority of the individuals have found a balance within and an authenticity to live their own lives from. Imagine a world where most of the people you encounter are enjoying their lives, not complaining bitterly about them. Imagine being proactive and passionate, having purpose and meaning in your life. Imagine other people being as passionate about their purpose as well, and that all is working together in this connected web we call life.

Imagine being one of those people you see on television or read about in books and call "hero." What we do on an individual scale reaches out like the ripples on the surface of a pond, touching everyone we come into contact with. The influence we have to make a better world is greater than we can imagine.

We all have the capacity to be more authentic, powerful individuals and we have the ability to change our world because of our own transformations. Even though it has been easier up to this point for many of us to remain stuck in mediocrity, safe in our comfort zones, cozy in our embedded beliefs and deep-seated denials, the challenges of the world may be pressing upon us to take the more difficult path to self-awareness and self-empowerment. In fact, our world may depend upon it.

Amidst political, economic, and social strife, and the threats of environmental devastation, it becomes easy to fall back into "victim" status and to let the "villains" have their way. The order of the day is hatred, greed, corruption, and the hopelessness of the people forced to live in less than ideal conditions so that a few can benefit. The attitude is often one of deep hopelessness and loss, grief and despair, and weakness because we have been taught to look at ourselves as "slaves to the rich and powerful," "worker drones," and "rats on a wheel." However, we don't have to keep buying into the symbols of a world out of balance. We can change, but we first have to change our own beliefs and symbols, our archetypes, behaviors, and stories. We are all each a chapter in a book made up of billions of chapters, but it must be read as the whole of humanity if it is to survive. One way to assure that is for as many of those chapters to work toward the desired plotline of the greater good. We are the chapters.

Just as we hope to stop being weak and find our inner "lion," or stop acting so foolish and bring out the inner "sage," the world around us is crying out for more empowering archetypes to represent the highest and best it can be. Maybe we can become a little less "warmaker" and a lot more "peacemaker." But it first begins at home with each of us removing the aspects of ourselves that make us angry, violent, greedy, narcissistic, abusive, and negative; or at least balancing the "innocent" with the "shadow" aspects of the self enough to create the fertile ground for a harmonious planet, one person and one archetype at a time.

So when the call to adventure comes, take it. Gather your courage, open your heart to cross that threshold into the unknown, and keep an eye out for your allies and mentors. Don't be afraid when you come to the challenges and the abyss, no matter how scary, dark, and deep it may appear to be. There are forces coming to your aid and friends to help you face the darkness that must be faced before you can become a warrior, a survivor, and a hero. Take the task with everything you have and proudly claim your reward. Thank those who have helped you and recognize the inner forces that have been driving your destiny. Take your reward and begin the long walk home.

The end result, once you journey back home, is a better life not just for you, but for your loved ones, your neighbors, and everyone you come in contact with. This world can use more heroes, more dreamers, and more lovers and bringers of light.

Go be one. There is nothing stopping you but the stories you tell yourself and the symbols you choose to identify with. Look inside. There's a "lion" in there. Let it roar!

[conclusion]

Been There, Done That

As the author of this book, I have some power. I'm a creator. Right now, I want to exercise the inner teacher, leader, guide, and mentor and tell you, dear readers, why it was so important to me to write this book at this time. It might be a little unorthodox to suddenly begin writing in the first person, but one of my archetypes is "rebel." I wear that badge proudly.

At my age, having been through many decades of life and experience, I realized that most, if not all, of my own unhappiness came from how I saw myself and how I projected that out into the world. My patterns of belief were, to put it simply, killing me. The real me. I am not going to tell my life story here and bore you to tears because we all have our stories and they are all fascinating and unique. But a series of events during the last 20 years really became a prolonged "wake-up call" for me to take real action and figure out why I kept having the same damn problems over and over and over again.

I hit rock bottom. I had *enough*.

So I began the hard work of change. I changed a lot of things on the surface of my life, and a few that I realized were inside jobs. But still, those patterns persisted. Hadn't I already come to understand my patterns? Wasn't I consciously aware of them now? So why did they keep showing up, undermining and sabotaging my happiness and success in all areas of my life? *Why?*

I wasn't digging deep enough. Oh, I had done the inner child healings and read all the John Bradshaw books. I thought I had gone deep enough to identify things that happened in my childhood and traced them to current, adult behaviors and patterns. I thought I knew what I was doing by taking classes and reading books about self-empowerment until my eyes bulged. But it wasn't enough.

Doing work on the surface can only go so far. Changing the external can only go so far. Even physically removing myself from a particular person or situation only went so far. In the recovery movement it's called "pulling a geographic" because basically all we are doing is changing our location and bringing with us the same baggage that weighed us down before. It's not enough. Think about a road full of potholes that finally gets filled, but below is a giant sinkhole just waiting to swallow up everything within a mile radius. Imagine moving 10, 15 times, as I did, and each time realizing after that initial "honeymoon" glow of a new place with new rooms that I had taken all my damn unwanted baggage with me.

So I had to do the inner work, and I really thought I had. Unfortunately, I had only been willing to go so far and then I just hit a wall. Call it the wall of denial or ignorance. Call it just plain being afraid to dig too deep for fear I might fall into the hole I was digging. After more years of the same patterns tearing me apart and keeping me from fully being alive and happy, I figured I needed a bigger shovel.

For the last 10 years, my own life has seen many archetypes come to the surface that I had no idea were governing my thoughts, beliefs, and actions. Through a number of awful, traumatic situations I got to meet some of them face-to-face, and I could no longer deny they were within me, operating at that deep collective unconscious level. And here's the thing—once you see something with full clarity, you can never "unsee" it. If you continue to deny it, the universe has this wonderful way of reminding you with even more experiences that trigger those rotten patterns and rile up those negative archetypes.

I was still, much to my chagrin, identifying myself all the time with being a "victim." Even though other aspects of my life seemed to portray a woman of courage and vision and even though I was doing many things others feared doing, I was still, in my heart, a "victim." No matter how hard I worked and what great work I put out into the world, all I was doing was drawing more people and situations into my life to prove that I was a—you guessed it—"victim"!

Then I hit bottom. And you know what? I got so damn sick and tired of being a victim, I changed. It didn't happen overnight, but it did happen. It didn't mean I would never be victimized again, because I was. But once I hit that point where I just couldn't take another day of being treated like a doormat, taken for granted, taken advantage of, and betrayed, I told the inner "victim" to pack her bags and go take up house elsewhere.

There was a new kid coming to town: "warrior."

Is my life perfect now? Heck no, I still have a lot of work to do going after my goals and dreams, helping my son grow into a good man who loves his life and lives his dreams, and being the kind of person I envision and know is the "real me." This work doesn't end, because we are continually growing into newer versions of ourselves.

But now, every time I start to feel the "victim" sneak into my sacred house again, I have the power and the tools to slam the door shut and instead bring out my "warrior." I stand tall and proud and remind myself what I've been through, and that I can take on any challenge that comes my way as long as I operate from more powerful places than I did before. I remember that I survived some pretty awful things and lived to tell about it. I act "as if" and become a better, more authentic version of myself. Or if I am just not up to being my warrior spirit, I can call in my "goddess" or "queen" to remind me what a badass I am! If I can do this, anyone can.

Nothing will ever erase the past and many people have pasts filled with major abuse, trauma, and suffering that is still, to this day, holding them back and causing them suffering and pain. But living a half-life is not the answer. Being haunted by old ghosts is not the answer. Denying the trauma of the past is not the answer. We all deserve happiness today, regardless of the past. If this book can help even one person find a way to replace old archetypal patterns and identities with empowering new ones, then I consider myself a real "mentor" and "guide."

As I look at the world around me, it would be easy to focus on the horrors that abound. The negative is everywhere. "Villains" are afoot, working their dark magic. But focusing on the bad does the world no good. Instead, I can take what I've learned about myself, express aspects that are positive and empowering to everyone around me, and try to be an example of a "hero" for my son, who represents the "prince," "visionary," and maybe even one of the "saviors" of the next generations.

Until each of us improves our own identity of who we are and begins to express authenticity and truth within our own minds, projecting it outward into the world, things on a grander scale will continue to be a reflection of the majority of those who simply aren't happy, whole, and fulfilled. Look around. I know you know these sad souls. Maybe you are one of them?

Remember that song about letting there be peace in the world and how it first has to begin with you? The same applies to using archetypes to empower our lives. If we do the individual work, we will stop being riddled with so much baggage from the past, which frees us up to be more present, awake, and aware to what is happening all around us. Our energy shifts and our vibration changes. We no longer feel helpless to do anything to help our planet because we no longer feel helpless about helping ourselves.

So don't be afraid to clean up your consciousness, but don't forget while you are at it to also clean up your subconscious and the archetypes you project into the collective unconscious. What you put into that collective unconscious matters not just to you and your own life, but to everyone else who exists now, has ever existed, or will exist in the future. Yep, that's some incredible responsibility, isn't it? To realize that by improving your own little backyard, you improve more of the collective planet we all exist on. We are all interconnected. You wouldn't want to be "that house" in your neighborhood, would you?

Making the world a better place is a work in progress. But it really does begin with me making me a better me and with you making you a better you.

One of my all-time favorite songs is called "Listen to the Lion" by Van Morrison. You could call it my "fight song." Whenever I need to remember who I am and how far I've come, I simply turn within and listen to the "lion" inside of me. Rawr!

[notes]

Introduction

1. Merriam-Webster Online, *http://Merriam-Webster.com/dictionary/archetype*.

Chapter 1

1. Brian Tracy, *http://briantracy.com*.
2. Ibid.
3. Encyclopedia of Philosophy, *http://iep.utm.edu.freud*.
4. Ibid.
5. Simply Psychology, *http://simplypsychology.org/sigmund-freud.html*.

6. Ibid.

7. *Encyclopedia Britannica, http://britannica.com/biography/ Carl-Jung.*

8. Ibid.

9. Carl G. Jung, *The Archetypes and the Collective Unconscious* (New York, New York: Bollingen Press, 1959).

10. Ibid.

11. Ibid.

Chapter 2

1. Heinrich Robert Zimmer and Joseph Campbell, *Philosophies of India* (New York, New York: Princeton University Press, 1969).

2. John Locke, *Essay Concerning Human Understanding* (London, England: William Tegg Press, 1689).

3. Aristotle, *De Anima*, Internet Classics Archive, *http://classics.mit/edu/Aristotle/Soul.1.html.*

4. "Research Decodes Ancient Celtic Astronomy Symbols and Links to Jungian Archetypes," Ancient-Origins.net, *http://ancient-origins.net.*

5. Miranda J. Green, *Dictionary of Celtic Myth and Legend* (London, England: Thames and Hudson, 1997).

6. St. Augustine, *De Deversis Questionibus*, *http://textmanuscripts.com/medieval/augustine-confessiones.*

7. Carl G. Jung, *The Archetypes and the Collective Unconscious* (New York, New York: Bollingen Press, 1959).

Chapter 3

1. Nicholas Goodrick-Clarke, *Black Sun: Aryan Cults, Esoteric Nazism, and the Politics of Identity* (New York: New York University Press, 2003).
2. Caroline Myss, *http://myss.com/blog.*
3. Caroline Myss, *Sacred Contracts: Awakening Your Divine Potential* (New York, New York: Three River Press, 2002).
4. Caroline Myss, *http://myss.com/blog.*
5. Ibid.
6. Carl G. Jung, ed., *Man and His Symbols* (New York, New York: Dell Publishing, 1968).
7. Wilfred L. Guerin, *A Handbook of Critical Approaches to Literature* (London, England: Oxford University Press, 2010).
8. Deborah Rudd, "Examples of Archetypes, Literature," *http://billstifler.org/en111/archetype.html.*
9. *Satapatha Brahmana*, Sacred Texts Online, *http://sacred-texts.com.*
10. "Chinese Myths," *http://livingmyths.com/Chinese.htm.*
11. Sigmund Freud, *The Interpretation of Dreams, http://verywell.com/the-interpretation-of-dreams.html.*
12. Carl G. Jung, ed., *Man and His Symbols* (New York, New York: Bollingen Press, 1959).
13. Ibid.

Chapter 4

1. M.L. von Franz, *Man and His Symbols* (New York, New York: Bollingen Press, 1959).
2. Thomas Singer, ed., *The Vision Thing: Myth, Politics and Psyche in the World* (New York, New York: Routledge Press, 2000).

3. Joseph Campbell, *The Hero with a Thousand Faces* (New York, New York: New World Library, 2008).

4. Christopher Vogler, *A Practical Guide to Joseph Campbell's 'The Hero with a Thousand Faces,'* *http://thewritersjourney. com/hero's_journey.htm.*

5. Joseph Campbell, *The Hero with a Thousand Faces* (New York, New York: New World Library, 2008).

6. John Shelton Lawrence and Robert Jewett, *The American Monomyth: Myth of the American Superhero* (New York, New York: Anchor Press, 1977).

Chapter 5

1. *The Big Book of Alcoholics Anonymous* (Alcoholics Anonymous World Service, 2002), 64.

2. Carl Greer, *Change Your Story, Change Your Life* (Scotland: Findhorn Press, 2014).

Chapter 6

1. Dawn Romeo, *Change Your Story, Change Your Life* (Kindle Publishing Services, 2016).

2. Michelle Fondin, "What Is a Chakra?" Chopra.com, *http://chopra.com/articles/what-is-a-chakra#sm.000066e0s8c dndyjv2112lhjwm5wf.*

3. Jean Shinoda Bolen, *Goddesses in Everywoman: Powerful Archetypes in Women's Lives* (New York, New York: Harper Perennial Books, 1984).

4. Ibid.

Chapter 7

1. *Chinese Astrology Online, http://chineseastrologyonline.com.*

2. Carol Allen, *The Five Astrological Archetypes of Relationships, http://loveisinthestars.com.*

3. Patrick McNamara, "Can Our Dreams Solve Problems While We Sleep?" *Psychology Today*, April 15, 2014.

4. "Nightmares in Adults," *Dream Interpretation Dictionary*, *http://dreaminterpretationdictionary.com/nightmares-in-adults.html*.

5. "Lucid Dreaming," *Dream Interpretation Dictionary*, *http://dreaminterpretationdictionary.com/lucid-dreaming-techniques.html*.

6. Jean Shinoda Bolen, *Goddesses in Everywoman: Powerful Archetypes in Women's Lives* (New York, New York: Harper Perennial, 1984).

Chapter 8

1. Heatherash Amara, *Warrior Goddess Training: Become the Woman You Are Meant to Be* (San Antonio, Texas: Hierophant Books, 2014).

2. Ibid.

3. Caroline Myss, *Sacred Contracts: Awakening Your Divine Potential* (New York, New York: Three Rivers Press, 2002).

[bibliography]

Allen, Carol. *The Five Astrological Archetypes of Relationships*. *http://loveisinthestars.com*.

Amara, Heatherash. *Warrior Goddess Training: Become the Woman You Are Meant to Be*. San Antonio, Texas: Hierophant Publishing, 2014.

"Archetype," *http://literaryterms.net/archetype*.

"Archetypal Energy," *http://archetypalenergy.com/archetypes*.

Bolen, Jean Shinoda. *Goddesses in Everywoman: Powerful Archetypes in Women's Lives*. New York, New York: Harper Perennial, 1984.

Campbell, Joseph. *The Inner Reaches of Outer Space: Metaphor as Myth and as Religion (The Collected Works of Joseph Campbell).* New York, New York: New World Library, 2012.

———. *The Hero with a Thousand Faces.* New York, New York: New World Library, 2008.

———. *The Symbol Without Meaning.* Joseph Campbell Foundation, 2013.

Campbell, Joseph, and Heinrich Zimmer. *The Philosophies of India.* Princeton, New Jersey: Princeton University Press, 1969.

Cherry, Kendra. "The Conscious and Unconscious Mind: The Structure of the Mind According to Freud." VeryWell.com, September 6, 2016.

Estes, Clarissa Pinkola. *Women Who Run With the Wolves: Myths and Stories of the Wild Woman Archetype.* New York, New York: Ballantine Books, 1996.

Falkenberg, Saffyre. "Jungian Archetypes in Pop Culture." Prezi.com, *http://prezi.com.* March 2015.

Fordham, Frieda, and Michael S.M. Fordham. "Carl Jung." *Encyclopedia Britannica, http://britannica.com/biography/Carl-Jung.*

Greer, Carl. *Change Your Story, Change Your Life: Using Shamanic and Jungian Tools to Achieve Personal Transformation.* Scotland, U.K.: Findhorn Press, 2014.

———. "7 Keys to Dream Interpretation," *http://carlgreer.com.*

Hillman, James. *The Soul's Code: In Search of Character and Calling.* New York, New York: Random House, 1996.

Hull, R.F.C. (Translator.) *The Portable Jung.* New York, New York: Penguin Books, 1976.

James, Matt. "Conscious of the Unconscious." *Psychology Today,* July 30, 2013.

Jones, Marie D. *PSIence: How New Discoveries in Quantum Physics and New Science May Explain the Existence of Paranormal Phenomena.* Pompton Plains, New Jersey: New Page Books, 2007.

Jones, Marie D., and Larry Flaxman. *The Grid: Exploring the Hidden Infrastructure of Reality.* San Antonio, Texas: Hierophant Publishing, 2014.

————. *Viral Mythology: How the Truth of the Ancients Was Encoded and Passed Down Through Legend, Art and Architecture.* Pompton Plains, New Jersey: New Page Books, 2014.

Jung, C.G. *The Archetypes and the Collective Unconscious.* (Translated by R.F.C. Hull.) New York, New York: Bollingen Press, 1968.

————. *Man and His Symbols.* New York, New York: Dell Publishing Co., Inc., 1964.

————. *Psychology of the Unconscious: A Study of the Transformations and Symbolisms of the Libido, A Contribution to the History of the Evolution of Thought.* Amazon Digital Services, 2002.

"Lucid Dreaming Techniques." *Dream Interpretation Dictionary,* http://dreaminterpretation-dictionary.com.

McLeod, Saul. "Carl Jung." *Simply Psychology,* http://simplypsychology.org/carl-jung.html.

McNamara, Patrick. "Can Our Dreams Solve Problems While We Sleep?" *Psychology Today,* http://psychologytoday.com/blog/dream-catcher/201404/can-our-dreams-solve-problems-while-we-sleep.

Myss, Caroline. *Archetypes: A Beginner's Guide to Your Inner-Net.* Carlsbad, CA: Hay House Publishing, 2013.

————. *Archetypes: Who Are You?* Carlsbad, CA: Hay House Publishing, 2013.

————. *Sacred Contracts: Awakening Your Divine Potential.* Harmony Publishing, 2003.

Romeo, Dawn. *Change Your Story, Change Your Life.* Amazon Digital Services, 2016.

Singer, Thomas. (Editor.) *The Vision Thing: Myth, Politics and Psyche in the World.* New York, New York: Routledge Press, 2000.

Vogler, Christopher. "The Writer's Journey." *http://thewritersjourney. com/hero's_journey.htm.*

———. *A Practical Guide to Joseph Campbell's "Hero with a Thousand Faces." www.thewritersjourney.com.*

"What Are Dreams?" *http://dreaminterpretation-dictionary.com/what-are-dreams.html.*

"What Do Dreams Do For Us?" *http://psychologytoday.com/blog/ the-literary-mind/200911/what-do-dreams-do-for-us.*

Wilson, Shelly. *28 Days to a New YOU.* Bluebird House Publications, 2013.

———. *Connect to the YOU Within.* Bluebird House Publications, 2013.

———. *Journey into Consciousness: One Woman's Story of Spiritual Awakening.* Bluebird House Publications, 2013.

"Working With Archetypes." *http://OpeningSacredSpace.wordpress.com.*

"Working With Archetypes in Tarot." *http://planetwaves.net/news/ reading-tarot/working-with-the-archetypes-in-tarot-what-how-and-why.*

[index]

[about the author]

Marie D. Jones is the best-selling author of *Destiny vs. Choice: The Scientific and Spiritual Evidence Behind Fate and Free Will*, *2013: The End of Days or a New Beginning?: Envisioning the World After the Events of 2012*, *PSIence: How New Discoveries in Quantum Physics and New Science May Explain the Existence of Paranormal Phenomena*, and *Looking for God in All the Wrong Places*. Marie coauthored with her father, geophysicist Dr. John Savino, *Supervolcano: The Catastrophic Event That Changed the Course of Human History*. She is also the co-author of *11:11 The Time Prompt Phenomenon: The Meaning Behind Mysterious Signs, Sequences, and Synchronicities*, *The Resonance Key: Exploring the Links Between Vibration, Consciousness, and the Zero Point Grid*, *The Déjà vu Enigma: A Journey Through the Anomalies of*

Mind, Memory, and Time, The Trinity Secret: The Power of Three and the Code of Creation, This Book Is From the Future: A Journey Through Portals, Relativity, Wormholes, and Other Adventures in Time Travel, and *Viral Mythology: How the Truth of the Ancients Was Encoded and Passed Down Through Legend, Art, and Architecture.*

She has an extensive background in metaphysics, cutting-edge science, and the paranormal and has worked as a field investigator for MUFON (Mutual UFO Network) in Los Angeles and San Diego in the 1980s and 1990s.

Marie has been on television, most recently on the History Channel's *Nostradamus Effect* series and *Ancient Aliens* series, and served as a special UFO/abduction consultant for the 2009 Universal Pictures science fiction movie, *The Fourth Kind.* She has been interviewed on hundreds of radio talk shows all over the world, including *Coast To Coast* AM, NPR, KPBS Radio, *Dreamland,* the *X-Zone, Kevin Smith Show, Paranormal Podcast, Cut to the Chase, Feet 2 The Fire, World of the Unexplained,* and the *Shirley MacLaine Show,* and has been featured in dozens of newspapers, magazines, and online publications all over the world. She is a former staff writer and official blogger for Jim Harold's *Paranormal Braintrust* and has written regularly for *Intrepid Magazine, Atlantis Rising, MindScape, Paranormal Underground, New Dawn Magazine,* and *Paranoia Magazine.* She has been a past radio host for Dreamland Radio and ParaFringe Radio.

She has lectured at major metaphysical, paranormal, new science, and self-empowerment events, including "Through the Veil," "Queen Mary Weekends," "TAPS Academy Training," "CPAK," and "Paradigm Symposium," "Conscious Expo," and "Darkness Radio Events," on the subjects of cutting-edge science, the paranormal, metaphysics, noetics, and human potential. She is also a screenwriter and producer with several projects in development. She has also taught a women's workshop through BBA, a 12-step program of recovery for addiction and codependency issues. Her websites are *www.mariedjones.com* and *www.whereslucyproductions.com.*